How to Hear the Voice of God in a Noisy World

Teresa Seputis

Charisma
HOUSE

HOW TO HEAR THE VOICE OF GOD IN A NOISY WORLD
by Teresa Seputis
Published by Charisma House
A part of Strang Communications Company
600 Rinehart Road
Lake Mary, Florida 32746
www.charismahouse.com

Unless otherwise noted, all Scripture quotations are from the New King James Version of the Bible. Copyright © 1979, 1980, 1982 by Thomas Nelson, Inc., publishers. Used by permission.

Scripture quotations marked NAS are from the New American Standard Bible. Copyright © 1960, 1962, 1963, 1968, 1971, 1972, 1973, 1975, 1977 by the Lockman Foundation. Used by permission. (www.Lockman.org)

Scripture quotations marked NIV are from the Holy Bible, New International Version. Copyright © 1973, 1978, 1984, International Bible Society. Used by permission.

Library of Congress Catalog Card Number: 2001086028
International Standard Book Number: 0-88419-755-7

01 02 03 04 05   8 7 6 5 4 3 2 1
Printed in the United States of America

Acknowledgments

- I would like to thank Jim Wies, who has been available to me for mentoring and advice over the years. Jim has affected my thinking and helped me to fine-tune my own hearing of God's voice. I sure appreciate you, Jim!

- I would also like to acknowledge John Webster, who provided very helpful insights and advice during an important growth period in my life.

- Some of the ideas and concepts I carry were picked up from Christian International, which provides much excellent training in the area of hearing God's voice.

- Another big influence on my thinking comes from one of my Fuller Seminary professors, C. Peter Wagner. I have sat under him in several classes, and what he taught has molded my thinking and worldview. Peter's insights on intercession, intimacy with God and spiritual warfare have greatly influenced my own growth in the Lord and my ability to hear God's voice. In fact, Peter was the first one to teach me that it is possible for intercessors to come before God and receive direction from Him on how He wanted me to pray. That was a major breakthrough in my own personal learning to hear and recognize God's voice for myself.

I have not intentionally lifted any ideas or concepts without giving credit to the source. If any of the material presented in my book resembles these sources, it is because they have been a big influence on my life and thinking. I want to acknowledge them and give credit and thanks to them up front.

Contents

ONE

You Can Know God's Voice

I work in San Francisco's financial district, the downtown area of a "big city" where parking is expensive and difficult to find. Most of us who work in the city commute in via public transportation. This type of commuting is a regular part of my life. God likes to meet us and speak to us in our everyday lives, so He frequently speaks to me about my commute.

For example, just two days ago I had to run an errand across town, so I took the bus. As I stepped out of the lobby, I could see the bus stop down the block on the other side of the street. The bus was just pulling up to the stop, and I knew I'd never make it in time. Nevertheless, I put forth a good effort and hurried toward the bus stop, but the bus pulled away before I ever crossed the street. I sighed, knowing that I'd have at least a twenty-minute wait for the next bus. I was about to sit down and make myself comfortable when God broke into my commute.

"Don't sit down, Teresa," He said. "The next bus will be here in less than five minutes."

That statement went against my natural knowledge of commute patterns. The buses typically ran twenty minutes apart at this time of day. I wanted to discount what I heard and to assume it was not really God's voice, but my own imagination or wishful thinking.

"Right, God," I found myself saying. "We both know the buses are spaced about twenty minutes apart."

"Look at your watch," the Lord replied.

I still was not 100 percent positive it was He who was speaking to me, but that sounded like something He would say. Even if it were not really God, it would not cost me anything to obey that directive, so I looked at my watch. It was eight minutes to the hour.

"The next bus will be here by five minutes to the hour," the Lord said. "Watch and see."

That phrase "watch and see" is something God often uses with me when I am not sure that it is He speaking to me as opposed to my own imagination. So I thought to myself, *OK, I will know whether or not this is God by whether or not the bus shows up in the next three minutes.* But I really did not expect the bus to come in that time frame.

Now God can hear my thoughts to myself as easily as He can hear my silent prayers and conversations with Him. He elected to comment on my thought. "Yes, Teresa, the bus will arrive in the time frame I have given, and then you will know you are hearing Me accurately. And then I have something I want to discuss with you. I am using this bus situation so that you will have confidence in your hearing for what I want to say to you next."

YOU CAN KNOW GOD'S VOICE

I spent the next sixty seconds wondering if the bus would actually show up in the time frame that I thought I'd heard God tell me. Then I looked up the street and saw a bus approaching. I really should not have been surprised, but I was, and my mouth fell open. I glanced at my watch, and it was six minutes to the hour. The bus pulled in front of me and opened its doors at precisely five minutes to the hour—just as God had said it would!

"Close your mouth," the Lord said, "and get on the bus. I want to talk to you about something. Now you know this is really My voice you are hearing." I did as He suggested. He had much more to say to me on the bus. I was so intently absorbed in our conversation that I almost missed my exit. God had to remind me I was at my destination and that it was time to get off the bus.

The next day I shared this experience with a friend. Her reply was, "I wish God would speak to me like He speaks to you!"

"Oh, He wants to!" I replied.

Then she said, "Well, I wish I could hear Him as clearly as you do."

"You can," was my instant reply.

You see, God wants to speak clearly and be understood clearly by each one of His children. He does not have any favorites. He desires to speak to each of us. He desires to meet us in our everyday lives and speak to us about them. He desires to speak to us about the big things, and about the little things as well. He wants to be involved in every area. He wants us to know His voice clearly so He can speak to us in a detailed manner. If you are a child of God, if you have been born again and if you belong to Jesus, then you can hear

God speak to you clearly. God desires His communication with us to be a normal part of our Christian walk. The purpose of this book is to help you learn how to discern and recognize His voice.

Some people think that God only wants to be involved in the big stuff and that we should not bother Him with the little stuff of everyday life. They feel that much of their day-to-day life is too unimportant to bother God with. But nothing could be further from the truth. God delights to be involved in every area of our lives. He likes to use the routine, day-to-day stuff as a training ground. He wants to give us confidence in His ability to communicate with us, so that when the big stuff comes along, we can know with a certainty that we are hearing from Him.

Let me share an example of God's involvement in everyday life. Ed and I don't have any children, but we have two dogs that we love dearly. They usually stay out for an hour every morning to do their "doggie business." One day, ten minutes after they went out, God told me to bring them back inside. That was out of the routine, but I have learned it is a very good idea to obey God when He tells us something.

So I went downstairs, opened the front door and called the dogs. They had gotten out of the yard and into the street. We live on a straight part of a mountain road, and cars often come whizzing past our house very fast. Dogs in the street have a very short life expectancy. Fortunately, there were no cars at the moment, and I got them safely inside.

The Lord knew my dogs are precious to me, so He alerted me to a potentially dangerous situation. God likes to come into our everyday lives and make them better.

RECOGNIZING GOD'S VOICE

Unfortunately we don't always listen to Him. Sometimes we don't listen because we have not yet learned how to recognize His voice. Sometimes we can hear Him, but we choose to ignore Him.

I did not always know how to recognize God's voice. God was always willing and able to speak to me, but I was totally clueless and did not know how to recognize His voice. But He taught me to know His voice. I was not a particularly adept learner, but He is an excellent teacher, so I learned. Chances are that it will be easier for you to learn to recognize and discern God's voice than it was for me. If I could do it, you can certainly do it, too!

Now, God speaks to me all the time. Sometimes He teaches me. Sometimes He explains things to me. Sometimes He gives me detailed instructions. Sometimes He just tells me how much He loves me. Occasionally He even teases me or lovingly plays a joke on me. I am not special. God does not speak to me because I am a minister, because I am holier than anyone else (I'm not!) or because I am important (I'm not!). He speaks to me for one simple reason: God loves to communicate with His children, and I am His child. The only reason I hear Him more clearly than many is because I took Him up on His offer to teach me to hear His voice.

He is extending that same offer to you right now. You can learn to recognize God's voice. It is a process—it takes time. But He will be with you every step of the way. And if you are willing, God would love for you to hear Him as clearly as you hear a friend standing beside you and talking to you. He really does intend communication with Him to be a normal part of your Christian experience. And He wants to teach you how to recognize when He speaks to you.

God spoke to Samuel when he was a child serving in the temple. (See 1 Samuel 3:1–14.) At that time, Samuel did not know it was God speaking to him. Instead he ran to Eli when God called his name and said, "Here I am, for you called me" (1 Sam. 3:5). Poor Samuel got it wrong three times. You would think God might have gotten frustrated with him and given up.

But God is a faithful and patient teacher. Instead, He came a fourth time and called Samuel's name. This time it was different. Why? Because Samuel had been given some instructions about how to hear God's voice. Eli had told him how to respond to the Lord. Suddenly the young and untrained boy was involved in a conversation with God Almighty.

If you have tried to hear God's voice in your past and failed, I have good news for you. The Lord has sent you an Eli in the form of this book to teach you how to respond to God and position yourself to hear from Him and recognize His voice. He wants to teach you, and He will do it if you cooperate with Him.

You see, God wants to speak clearly to you even more than you desire to hear Him! He is willing to teach you how to recognize His voice. He is capable of teaching you and communicating clearly to you even though you may get it wrong or mishear His voice when you first begin. So the onus is on God—not on you.

God is interested in watching out for you. He wants to take care of every detail of your life—the big things and the small things. He wants to speak into every area of your life—from your leisure activities to work-related items to major life decisions. He wants to show you His will clearly in each situation and empower you to walk in it.

GOD WANTS TO
COMMUNICATE WITH US

God is a communicating God, and He wants to communicate directly with each of us. He wants to meet us where we are...to reveal Himself to us and to change any misconceptions we have of what He is really like. As Jesus said in John 10:4, as His sheep it should be a normal part of our Christian experience to hear and know His voice.

There is just one thing I need to warn you about. God has a great deal of warmth and a rich sense of humor. Some people envision God as always staunch and stern. They miss some of what He has to say, because He does not always sound just the way we think He should sound. Sometimes He can be a bit of a tease.

We are created in God's image and have a sense of humor. (At least most of us do!) We should not think it strange that God has one, too. He has pulled many jokes on me. Let me share my favorite with you.

During the famous *El Niño* weather pattern recently, here in the San Francisco Bay area we had day after day of rain for nearly three months. One day in the midst of all that rain, I had to take my $3,000 laptop computer to work with me. My daily commute includes lots of outdoor walking—rain or shine.

It had been raining every day for the past month. I was not thrilled about taking my laptop, as computers do not like to get wet. But I had no choice. So I grabbed my laptop and my umbrella and started out the door to my car.

"Teresa," the Lord said, "it is not going to rain today. You don't need your umbrella."

"Lord," I replied, "it is small and light. I don't mind taking it."

"Teresa, I just told you it is not going to rain. I want you to leave your umbrella at home."

I pondered the weather pattern over the past weeks. "Lord," I said, "I would really rather take my umbrella along."

"No, Teresa," He replied. "I want you to trust Me and leave the umbrella at home. Will you obey Me on this?"

When He put it that way, I really did not have much of a choice. Reluctantly I put the umbrella down and said, "OK, God, I am trusting You. You are promising that it won't rain today at all, right, God?"

"That is what I said. It will not rain today."

I made it all the way to work with no rain. It seemed that maybe I'd heard God right after all and it really would not rain! I was working at my desk on the eighth floor of a skyscraper. Suddenly there was the pitter-patter of water drops against my window. I looked out to see raindrops landing on my window.

"Lord!" I gasped, "You told me it was not going to rain today!"

"Teresa," God said, "it is not raining."

"Then I suppose those aren't really raindrops hitting my window?"

"Trust Me, it is not raining."

Everything inside of me wanted to scream out, "Oh come on, God, who are You trying to kid?" Instead, I took a deep breath, swallowed and said, "OK, Lord, if You say so, I guess it's not raining."

"It's not. Here, let Me show you." Just then a window washer let himself down in front of my window and waved at me. I nearly jumped out of my chair with surprise, when he came down so fast and so suddenly. What had looked like rain was really water drops from when he'd been washing the windows on the floor above me.

God had been right after all. It really was not raining. I will never forget what God said next. In a teasing voice He said, "Gotcha!"

POINTS TO PONDER

1. Have there been times when God has gotten involved in your day-to-day life, turning a potentially negative situation around for His glory?

2. Have you ever had an experience where you believe God spoke clearly and specifically to you?

3. Have there been times when you think God may have been speaking to you, but you were not sure whether or not it was really His voice? Would you like to know His voice more clearly?

4. Have there been times when you believed God was speaking to you, but you intentionally chose not to obey Him on it? What was the result of not listening to God?

TWO

God Is a Communicating God

One of the things I have noticed is that God seems to be a whole lot less concerned about our theology than we are about each other's. I have heard the theology of some people—which I was certain was in error—yet God has used those people powerfully. When I asked God about it, He said, "Oh, I am not at all worried about the fine points of their theology. As they get to know Me better, I will reveal more of Myself to them. In that way I will correct their misconceptions about Me."

When He gave me that answer, I should have known that His answer applied to my own theology as well. I thought I knew God pretty well at that time, and I thought I had a very solid theology. But I have discovered that God is constantly breaking out of whatever theological boxes I have put Him into. There are some basic doctrines that remain absolutely unwavering—

such as salvation is available only through the blood of Jesus. But when it comes to understanding the nature and character of God, He is constantly showing me that I still have some misconceptions about who He is. We all do.

MISCONCEPTIONS ABOUT GOD

The problem with misconceptions about God is that they can interfere with our relationship with Him. They can hold us back in various areas. For instance, someone who sees God the Father as distant, unloving and hard to please will have great difficulty entering into intimacy with Him.

There are misconceptions that interfere specifically with our ability to hear God's voice. These misconceptions convey one of two messages:

- "God does not speak directly to His children today."

- "God does speak to His children today, but He doesn't want to speak to me personally."

We phrase our misconceptions so that they sound spiritual or more acceptable. For instance, you may hear people say, "God wrote the Bible. He won't say anything to us today because He expects us to go get it directly from the Bible." Well, that is partially true. The Bible is the absolute Word of God and is the standard by which we judge all else. But the Bible itself leads us to believe God still communicates personally and directly with His children.

God does not change (Mal. 3:6). God will never say something today that contradicts what He has already spoken in His Word, the Bible. But God has not developed laryngitis, and He still speaks directly to His children today, just as the Bible indicates He does.

Other common misconceptions are that a person must be extremely devout or holy to be able to hear God, or that some people are incapable of hearing God. Some even believe that God speaks only in a cryptic and hard-to-understand manner, like some sort of mystic oracle or divine code.

I want to address these misconceptions up front. They are dangerous and can keep us from learning to recognize God's voice.

The truth is that God is a communicating God who enjoys talking with His children. In fact, He specifically created us with ears to hear His voice: "The hearing ear and the seeing eye, the LORD has made both of them" (Prov. 20:12, NAS). God created us with an innate ability to hear Him—because He wants to communicate with us. He still speaks frequently and clearly to His children today, and He expects us to be able to hear and comprehend His voice (John 10:27).

The Bible offers a great deal of support for the above premises. Let's go back to the very beginning and look at God's initial creation—Adam and Eve. The Bible makes it clear that both Adam and Eve possessed the ability to hear God from the first day they were created. First God created man and woman. Then on the very day He created them *He began talking to them* (Gen. 1:27–28).

Right from the start, human beings had the ability to hear God speak to them. They could recognize and understand His voice. Why? Because God created them to fellowship with Him. God established His pattern of speaking directly to His children on day one. On that first day of created life, God established the manner by which He intended to proceed to speak to human beings, communicating clearly with them.

In fact, Genesis 3:8 suggests that God had the habit of walking in the garden and talking with Adam and Eve in the "cool of the day," or on a regular daily basis, probably just before sunset when it started to cool down.

Even after Adam and Eve fell into sin, God still spoke to them. And they were still able to hear His voice! Look at Genesis 3:8–13:

> And they heard the sound of the LORD God walking in the garden in the cool of the day, and Adam and his wife hid themselves from the presence of the LORD God among the trees of the garden.
>
> Then the LORD God called to Adam and said to him, "Where are you?"
>
> So he said, "I heard Your voice in the garden, and I was afraid because I was naked; and I hid myself."
>
> And He said, "Who told you that you were naked? Have you eaten from the tree of which I commanded you that you should not eat?"
>
> Then the man said, "The woman whom You gave to be with me, she gave me of the tree, and I ate."
>
> And the LORD God said to the woman, "What is this you have done?"
>
> The woman said, "The serpent deceived me, and I ate."

Adam and Eve both heard God's voice in their sinful and unforgiven state. When they heard God, the guilt and shame of their sin caused them to flee from His presence. But even in their fallen state, we see God seeking them out and communicating with them. In fact, He is holding a two-way conversation with

13

them. Because God loves us, He will continue to try to communicate with us.

DOES GOD SPEAK TO UNBELIEVERS?

History records that it wasn't long after Adam and Eve's disobedience before God communicated with another person who was not walking in perfect holiness. Look at Cain. (See Genesis 4:4–7.) The offering Cain made to God was unacceptable. Yet God initiated a dialogue with Cain, basically telling Cain to stop pouting. God explained why Cain's offering was not accepted, and then He gave Cain a warning.

Cain was not doing well in His relationship with God. God was unwilling to accept the offering that Cain tried to present to Him. Why? Because Cain was attempting to approach God on his own terms instead of on God's terms. God will not accept people on any terms other than His own, as evidenced by the rejection of the offering. However, Cain was sincerely seeking God. So God actually met him and entered into a dialogue with him.

Cain, who was not accepted by the Lord, was able both to hear God's voice and to converse with God. God attempted to teach Cain the importance of approaching Him on His terms, rather than man's terms, by saying, "If you do well, will you not be accepted?" (Gen. 4:7). God remained unwavering that man must approach Him on His terms. (Even today the only way to approach God is through the atoning sacrifice of His Son, the risen Lord Jesus Christ.)

At the same time, God demonstrated that He was willing to communicate with a sincere seeker and to instruct Cain on how to approach Him. God actually gave Cain a warning, one intended to help him past a difficult trial and to get him into a right relationship with God: "If you do not do well, sin lies at the door. And its desire is for you, but you should rule over it" (v. 7). Unfortunately Cain did not heed God's warning or follow God's advice. When he murdered his brother in a fit of jealous rage, he moved from being a *sincere but misguided seeker* to being *an unforgiven sinner* (Gen. 4:8). Even in this fallen and unforgiven state, the Bible demonstrates that Cain could hear God. In fact, he entered into an interactive dialogue with God in Genesis 4:9–15. Cain had just committed a sin (murder), and he had not been forgiven for it. Yet in the midst of all that, as a sinful and unforgiven man, Cain was still able to hear God's voice. This example is evidence that the abil ity to hear God is not based on your personal holiness or on the caliber of your personal relationship with God.

John Webster says this about Cain:

> Here we have a murderer speaking to God, having a conversation with God. So you're not hearing God's voice because you're righteous. Now please understand me. Righteousness is a good thing, isn't it? God wants us to live a holy and upright life before Him, doesn't He? Absolutely. It's a very high priority to God for our lives, but it is not a basis for hearing God's voice. So it is greatly important, but it's not the reason that you hear God's voice.[1]

Does God still speak to unsaved people today as He did to Cain when he was a sincere seeker? Yes, He does. A friend, let's call her Sue, is Jewish by birth. She grew up in Chicago during an era when there was a great deal of open prejudice against Jews. As a teen, she was poorly treated on multiple occasions in the "name of

Christ." As a result, to this very day, she resists anything (no matter how good it is) that is done or offered in the name of Christ.

Sue has explored a lot of religions from Judaism to Hinduism to various forms of spiritualism and New Age. At one point she followed and worshiped a popular guru. However, in the midst of that, God spoke to her, and she heard Him. He told her that she must worship God, not people. The encounter with God was so real that she, at great personal cost, left the guru's community and abandoned the spiritual practices associated with that guru. Did that encounter with God convert her? No, not yet. She still believes that all paths lead to God, and she still rejects Jesus. Yet God still continues to speak to her and reveal Himself to her.

When Sue first told me that God speaks to her, I did not believe it. I did not think that God would speak clearly to unbelievers. However, God has spoken to Sue periodically over the past few years. And I believe that what He says to her is moving her closer to the place where she can truly know Him. She came from years of New Age training where followers are taught that there is no such thing as sin. As a result, she rejects the notion of sin and of personal holiness. Yet God speaks to her about personal holiness. She has always been an ethical person, but God began to speak to her about stealing. What was her crime? She sometimes took office supplies from work for her personal use, just as everyone else at her office did. (Taking company pens is a common practice in many offices these days; people do not think anything about it.) But God began to speak to Sue that she must not do this because it was stealing in His eyes. That word was not a residual from her New Age training—it directly contradicted it! God spoke to her about it, and she responded to Him. He has convicted her in other areas of personal holiness, just as He would a believer. God has spoken to Sue about His great love for her. She is definitely responding to His love—what rational human being would not? He has been giving her "success experiences" in hearing Him so that she will recognize His voice when He explains to her that all paths do not lead to God. I believe God is wooing Sue to Jesus. God will not violate Sue's free will, nor will she be allowed into heaven without accepting Christ. But He is speaking to her just as He did to Cain to show her the way to Him. And as an unsaved woman, she is capable of hearing His voice and responding to Him.

BIBLICAL EXAMPLES OF GOD'S COMMUNICATION TO HIS PEOPLE

God is a communicating God. In week three of Prophetic-School Training 101, the lesson states that "the Bible, both the Old and New Testament, is filled with illustrations of God's desire to speak to us whether we are righteous or unrighteous."[2] It also lists some examples of God speaking to His children or to others about His children. These include:

- Adam and Eve—Genesis 2:16; 3:8–10, 13, 17
- Cain—Genesis 4:6–7, 9–12, 15
- Enoch—Genesis 5:24
- Noah—Genesis 6:13; 7:1; 8:15–17; 9:1, 17
- Abraham—Genesis 12:1, 4, 7; 13:14; 15:1–9, 18; 17:1–3, 9, 15, 18–19, 22; 18:1, 13, 17, 20; 20:3–7; 21:12–13; 22:1–2, 15–18
- Hagar—Genesis 16:7–13; 21:17–18
- Rebekah—Genesis 25:23
- Isaac—Genesis 26:2, 24

- Jacob—Genesis 28:13; 31:3, 11–13; 35:1, 10–11, 15
- Laban—Genesis 31:24, 29
- Pharaoh—Genesis 41:28
- Israel (Jacob)—Genesis 46:2
- Joseph—Genesis 37:5
- Moses—Exodus 3:14
- Joshua—Joshua 5:14–15
- Samuel—1 Samuel 3:10–14
- David—1 Samuel 23:2
- Solomon—1 Kings 3:5
- Job—Job 38
- Balaam—Numbers 22:12, 35
- Elijah—1 Kings 19:12–13
- Joseph—Matthew 1:20–21
- Pilate's wife—Matthew 27:19
- Peter—Acts 10:3, 13
- Paul—Acts 9:3–4; 27:23–24
- John—Revelation 1:10–11[3]

In the first chapter of John, the Bible calls Jesus the "Word" of God: "In the beginning was the Word, and the Word was with God, and the Word was God" (John 1:1). A *word* is the basic element of communication. Words comprise phrases and sentences, and sentences convey meaning. Thus, words are the building block by which communication occurs. God communicates Jesus to us in John chapter 1 as the basis of communication itself—Jesus is *the Word*. This emphasizes the fact that God is a communicating God. He desires to communicate with us. His Son, Jesus, is the basic element of all that He seeks to communicate to us.

Jesus expects His followers (sheep) to hear His voice. He states, "My sheep hear My voice, and I know them, and they follow Me" (John 10:27). This verse equates *knowing* Jesus to *being able to recognize His voice.* If His sheep know His voice, the implication is clear that He talks to them.

LEARNING HOW TO HEAR

One Bible scholar pointed out to me that this verse refers to Jewish believers. Because he is a non-Jewish believer, he argued that he is excluded from being required to hear God's voice. He looked very smug and proud of himself as he stressed this point. I was not sure how to respond to him, but God whispered to me, "Point out verse 16 to him. That will nail him!" John 10:16 says, "And I have other sheep, which are not of this fold; I must bring them also, and they shall hear My voice; and they shall become one flock with one shepherd" (NAS). His smug look faded as he realized that John 10:27 applied to him, too. Jesus expects each of His followers to hear His voice and listen to Him—no exceptions.

Why is it, then, that so many believers do not know how to hear God's voice? Someone answered the question with this comment: "Because they don't bother to listen."

That response is only partially true. The reason most believers today don't know how to hear God's voice is because they don't realize that they can, so they haven't yet learned how to hear.

Baby birds don't know that they can fly, even though God created them explicitly to do so. The parent bird has to teach them how. The parent waits until the right time in the baby bird's physical development, until the bones in the wings have grown strong enough and the feathers have grown. Then the parent pushes the baby out of the nest.

Some baby birds do not learn to fly on the first push out of the nest. They squawk as they fall helplessly toward the ground. The parent bird watches them fall and listens to their frightened cries, but does not intervene immediately. Why? Because the parent wants the baby bird to learn to experience flight. If the baby bird gets dangerously close to the ground, the parent bird swoops down and catches the baby. Then it brings the baby back to the nest and gives it a brief rest. But soon it shoves the baby out of the nest again.

Some birds go through this training process several times before they learn to fly. But eventually they all learn. Imagine that! Birds are created explicitly to fly, but they don't automatically know how to do it. They have to be taught.

God created His children with an innate ability to hear His voice, just as He created the bird with an innate ability to fly. However, many of us have not yet learned how to hear God's voice. In fact, some of us do not even know that hearing His voice is an option. Some do not know that God will speak directly and personally to them, so they have not yet learned how to recognize His voice.

It may be that God is "pushing you out of the nest" right now, teaching you to "fly." Before today you may not have known that God wants to speak directly and personally to you. You may not have known that He created you with the innate ability to hear His voice. Or perhaps you knew these things intellectually, but you did not actually know how to go about the process of learning to recognize His voice. The following chapters will help you learn to recognize His voice and to hear Him for yourself.

POINTS TO PONDER

1. Do you personally know anyone who hears directly from God on a regular basis? Do you believe it is common for God to speak directly to the believers around you? Or do you believe that it would be unusual for God to speak to His followers?

2. Do you personally find it easy to hear and recognize God's voice?

3. Many people have no trouble believing that God will speak to His children today. But at the same time, they don't think that He will speak personally *to them*. Why do you think that is?

4. Do you want to learn to recognize and hear God more clearly? If so, why? If not, why not?

THREE

God Speaks to Us Through His Word

As a communicating God, God finds many ways to speak to His children. The most important and reliable way is through His written Word, the Bible. The Bible is the inspired Word of God, and it must be our absolute standard by which we judge all else. When God speaks directly to us, we bounce it off of the written Word of God. If we "hear" God say something directly to us that contradicts the Bible, then we must assume we have "heard wrong."

> God is not a man, that He should lie, nor a son of man that he should change his mind.
> —NUMBERS 23:19, NIV

God doesn't lie or change His mind. He tells us, "I the LORD do not change" (Mal. 3:6, NIV).

So we see that it would be inconsistent with God's character to speak something to us in the Bible, which we hold as absolute truth, and then later to change His mind about it and say something contradictory. He simply would not do that!

God speaks to us through the Bible in many different ways. The most obvious is by teaching us "His ways"— how to please Him, how He desires us to behave, what He is like.

> Show me Your ways, O LORD; teach me Your paths. Lead me in Your truth and teach me, for You are the God of my salvation.
>
> —PSALM 25:4–5

The Bible makes it easy to discern His will in many situations. He has made clear what His standards of holiness are. For instance, believers do not wake up each morning and pray for divine guidance as to whether or not God wants them to steal from someone that day. God has already made His opinion on stealing quite clear. The Bible says that we are to be honest and fair in our dealings with others and generous to the needy, and it tells us implicitly that we are not to steal.

DOING WHAT WE HEAR GOD SAY

Have you noticed that many times the hard part is not *discerning how God wants us to behave*—the hard part is actually *doing what we know God wants us to do!* The Bible makes God's standards of behavior very clear. But sometimes it is not easy to walk out God's will once we understand it.

Let me illustrate using the example of forgiveness. We know that God fully expects us to forgive those who wrong us, just as God has forgiven us. (See Matthew 6:14–15; 18:33–35; Mark 11:25.) Yet, when someone deeply hurts or betrays us, we find that it is not very easy to forgive truly and completely because our emotions are engaged. We make a conscious decision to forgive, but many of us struggle as we try to walk that decision out.

We choose to forgive because we know this is what God wants us to do. But the next day we struggle with it again. So we lay it on the altar and cry out to God for His help to forgive. Then a few days or a few weeks later we find ourselves struggling with forgiveness again.

Even after the will is engaged, it is not easy to forgive sincerely and completely the person who has utterly devastated us. This is why we need the Holy Spirit in our hearts. He helps us to understand what God wants, and then He transforms us and empowers us to do it.

God has revealed many of His characteristics to us through His written Word. These characteristics include the following:

- God is loving—1 John 4:16
- He is forgiving—Ephesians 4:32
- He is good—Exodus 34:6
- He is kind—Psalm 63:3
- He is patient—2 Peter 3:9
- He loves all of us—John 3:16
- He desires to give us good gifts—Matthew 7:7–11
- He hates sin—Jeremiah 44:4
- He expects us to obey Him—John 14:15

God has chosen to reveal quite a bit to us about His character and nature through His Word, which gives us a framework to know Him experientially. Knowing His characteristics gives us insight about how to behave or act in many different situations.

There are times when we as believers need to hear from God above and beyond what He has already revealed in His written Word. We need to hear Him for our specific situations. Fortunately, God loves to talk to us, to answer our questions, to share His heart with us and to tell us things. He will frequently address things that are very personalized to our situation, but He will never contradict Scripture in doing so.

A SPECIFIC WORD
FOR A SPECIFIC SITUATION

The Holy Spirit is capable of quickening a scripture to us at just the right time so that it serves as clear guidance for a present situation. He can meet us through Scripture to communicate clearly on a specific situation where we need to hear Him.

Let me share an example of how God used Scripture to meet me in a very difficult situation. In 1996 I participated in a three-week missions trip to India. We were to depart for India three days after Thanksgiving. My parents, both unsaved at the time, came over for Thanksgiving dinner. Dad looked unusually tired, but I had no idea that his health was very bad. We had our usual brief discussion during which I invited him to receive Jesus as his Savior, and he declined.

The next morning during devotions, the Lord instructed me to open my Bible to Psalm 21. I began reading, "You have given him his heart's desire, and have not withheld the request of his lips" (v. 2). God stopped me right there and asked me, "Teresa, what are the desires of your heart?"

That was easy. I had just seen my unsaved parents the day before, and my husband was not saved yet

either. So I answered Him, "Salvation of my household, Lord. Please don't let anyone in my immediate
family die without accepting Jesus first." The Lord
told me to bring the desire of my heart to Him in
prayer, and He would grant it. The Lord and I spent
quite a bit of time that morning praying and discussing
this request for household salvation.

I got on an airplane two days later and headed to
India. We were in a very rural part of India that could
not receive international calls. One night late into the
trip, we received a phone call from our message center.
My father had died a couple of days before, and my husband had been trying to reach me for two days to tell me
this news. He finally got through to the message center
and left a message for me. They were passing it on.

I was in shock. Could that possibly be correct? My
unsaved father dead? The message said he had died
unexpectedly from a heart attack, instantly and probably painlessly, with no advance warning. But just days
before I had been praying for household salvation.
When I had last seen him, he was unsaved and unre-
ceptive to the message of Christ.

I recommitted my allegiance to the Lord no matter
what happened, and then I began to cry. My dad was
dead? Living conditions where we were staying in India
were very crowded, but the people made space for me
to be alone for a bit to give me time to pray and process.
I asked the Lord what had happened to my father. Had
he accepted Jesus? Was he in heaven or in hell? But I
was emotionally distraught and unable to hear God
clearly. So I waited on Him for a bit, and then I grabbed
my Bible. I had no idea what I wanted to read, but I suddenly felt impressed to read John 14.

The chapter began with these words: "Do not let

your hearts be troubled. Trust in God; trust also in me. In my Father's house are many rooms; if it were not so, I would have told you" (John 14:1–2, NIV). It seemed like the words were custom-made for my situation, and I drew great comfort from them.

Again and again the Holy Spirit directed my attention to the phrase, "If it were not so, I would have told you." I did not understand what He meant by it, so I asked Him. Suddenly Psalm 21:2 came flooding back into my memory: "You have given him his heart's desire, and have not withheld the request of his lips."

The Lord reminded me of the conversation we had just before I left for India. In that conversation, He had asked me what the desire of my heart was, and I had replied, "The salvation of my household." Psalm 21:2, the verse on which God was focusing my thoughts, said God had granted me the desires of my heart.

Then the Holy Spirit brought back to my memory John 14:2: "If it were not so, I would have told you." I believed He was telling me that I could count on Him to answer the prayer He led me to pray that day. He seemed to be reassuring me that He would not let any of my immediate family die without accepting Jesus first—or He would have told me. That would mean that my father had accepted Jesus before he died and was in heaven at that very moment.

The thought was very comforting. But it seemed in direct conflict to the information I had been given. I knew Dad was not a Christian the last time I saw him, and that he had died instantly and unexpectedly. Right about then, God broke clearly into my thoughts and said, "Teresa, the information you got in the message was wrong. He did not die unexpectedly; he knew he was dying, and he accepted Jesus and is in heaven." As if in confirmation, one of the Indian pastors came to me with a prophecy that he did not understand. He assumed that since I was a missionary, my parents were both saved. He was surprised to hear God tell him to give me this message: "Rest assured that despite how the circumstances may appear, your father is with Me in heaven." I received a final confirmation when I got home. It turns out my father had seen his doctor after having some tests and was told he needed another heart bypass surgery, or he would be dead in two weeks. He elected not to have the surgery and decided not to tell my mother about this. He knew for almost two weeks that he was dying and had plenty of time to get right with God.

Neither Psalm 21:2 nor John 14:2 were written to address the question of "Did my unsaved relative accept Christ before dying?" But the Holy Spirit used these two verses to communicate an assurance of my father's salvation to me. And then He brought independent confirmation afterward through the prophecy and through the doctor's report.

The Holy Spirit sometimes uses a few verses like that to communicate something specific to us. He may quicken a whole passage of Scripture, or He may suddenly flood us with scriptures along a given theme. For instance, one time God wanted me to go on a long fast and pray for my city. In a two-week period, I tripped across just about every passage on fasting in the Bible. The verses on fasting seemed practically to jump off the page at me. I finally got the idea that God wanted me to fast and pray for my city.

Part of the Holy Spirit's job description is to quicken Scripture to you, bringing it to your remembrance. We see this in John 14:26, which says, "But the Helper, the Holy Spirit, whom the Father will send in My name,

He will teach you all things, and bring to your remembrance all things that I have said to you." Of course, when the Holy Spirit brings something to your remembrance, it implies that you have already put that scripture in your memory at an earlier time! This means that if we want God to speak to us through Scripture, we should facilitate the process by spending time in His Word, reading it, studying it and memorizing it.

MISUSING WHAT GOD SAYS TO US

We have already discussed that the Bible is the inspired Word of God and is reliable both to lead us and to give us a standard by which to judge all else we believe God says to us. We have seen that the Holy Spirit will sometimes quicken passages of Scripture to us or recall them to our memory when He desires to communicate something specific to us through Scripture. But as wonderful as the Scripture is, it is still possible for believers to *misuse* it.

This discussion would not be complete if I did not talk about two misuses in the area of hearing God speak through Scripture.

MANIPULATING SCRIPTURE

The first is trying to manipulate Scripture to say something God is not saying—putting words in His mouth. You may say, "But I would never do that!" Most of us would not intentionally do something like that. Yet the Bible warns us that "the heart is deceitful above all things, and desperately wicked" (Jer. 17:9).

Sometimes our unconscious mind wants something so badly that we find a scripture to twist to "fit our desire." Then we try to pretend God has promised it to us. Because we are not honest with ourselves, we begin to believe God really has promised it to us—when He has not. Perhaps the best way to illustrate this is to share a rather embarrassing example from my own past.

I was recently out of college and very single. It seemed that all the single Christian men I met fell into one of three categories—already dating someone else, very chauvinistic or weird. I was fairly attractive and always had a lot of unsaved men asking me out. The unsaved men did not seem to fall into any of the three categories. Yet I knew that 2 Corinthians 6:14, "Do not be unequally yoked together with unbelievers," meant I should not date unbelievers.

I turned to God for help. I began to pray that He would bring along the special man He had for me. At the time there was one man whom I liked who was a nominal Christian. He was about to leave the area to study for two years at Massachusetts Institute of Technology. I was more interested in having God meet my need for a boyfriend/spouse than I was with wanting to know what His will was for my life. In other words, I wanted it *my way!* I found a scripture that said, "Delight yourself also in the LORD, and He shall give you the desires of your heart" (Ps. 37:4). I interpreted that to mean that since I wanted a boyfriend/husband, God was obligated to give me one.

Somehow I took a giant leap. Stan and I were only casually dating at the time. But I reasoned that since I liked Stan, and he was leaving for MIT, Psalm 37:4 was promising me that Stan and I would get married as soon as he got back in two years.

As time progressed, it became clear that the "long-distance relationship" was not working. I was in California, and he was in Massachusetts, a very long way away. After about six months, Stan found himself a local girlfriend. I was devastated and could not understand how that could happen since I had God's promise in Psalm 37:4 that He would give me the desire of my heart. My desire was to marry—and I figured that meant Stan.

So my mind twisted things a little further. I calculated that I would be twenty-seven by the time the two years were up. I changed the promise to be that I would be married—probably not to Stan, though—before I turned twenty-eight. I claimed that promise, using Psalm 37:4 as my basis, and held on to it for dear life.

There was only one minor problem with this promise—God had never made it, and He had absolutely no intention of fulfilling it. Twenty-seven came and went, and I was still single. I remember sitting alone on my bed on Valentine's Day when I was twenty-eight, hugging my pillow and crying because I did not have a date.

I got mad at God for not keeping His promise (one He actually had never made). I told myself that if God would not take care of me, I would take care of myself. I began accepting the offers for dates from non-Christians. At first I only dated when it did not interfere with church, but after a while I made dating the priority and hardly attended church. Before long, God was no longer a very important part of my life—I hardly ever thought about Him. This was the start of a four-year-long backslide, during which time I met and married a wonderful but unsaved man.

God tried to speak to me about three days before the wedding. This experience was probably the most clearly I had ever heard God in my life up to that point. The Holy Spirit said to me, very distinctly, "Teresa, you know you are not supposed to be unequally yoked." I knew it was God. I was surprised and startled to hear His voice. But there was no way in the world I was going to call off this wedding. I was still mad at God for not keeping the promise—the one He had never really made. I told Him that I did not care what He wanted. He had not taken care of me, so I was going to take care of myself. I thought that if I could repent later, great. But if not…oh well…

Can you believe I actually said something like that to God? I was backslidden and very foolish at the time. I went through with the wedding in 1988, and Ed and I are still married. In many respects, I believe that Ed is the man God had for me. We are perfect for each other in many ways, and we love each other. The only problem was my timing. I now believe that if I had delayed the wedding and taken a stand about not being unequally yoked, Ed would have seriously taken a look at Christianity. I think God's plan was to get Ed saved—and then get us married. But since Ed got what he wanted (that is, me), he is not interested now in hearing the gospel. I still believe that he will eventually come to know the Lord, but my rebellion has certainly slowed down the process.

The reason I was so rebellious was because I had put words in God's mouth. I found a scripture that I twisted to "back up" the words I put in His mouth. Then I was hurt and angry when God did not keep the promise He had not made. Don't repeat my mistake. Don't do what I did! Do not try to modify Scripture to promise things that God is not really promising.

Using the Bible out of context

There is a second misuse of God's Word, which is using the Bible out of context, sort of like a horoscope.

Some Christians open the Bible each day and find whatever verse they first come across and think that is God's word for them for the day. The Bible is not a spiritual Ouija board, and we must not use it as such. There may be times when God brings a scripture to you sovereignly in a seemingly random manner. But don't look to that as a regular routine.

There is an old joke that illustrates the point: Someone was used to plopping open a Bible and taking the first verse he saw as guidance for the day. One day he opened to Matthew 27:5, which read, "He [Judas]... went and hanged himself." Thinking that was not a very good verse for the day, he tried again and opened to Luke 10:37, which read, "Jesus said to him, 'Go and do likewise.'" (I think you get the point!)

The devil tried to take Scripture out of context and misrepresent its meaning to Jesus. This is what happened when he tempted Jesus in the wilderness. Satan tried to twist Scripture and take it out of context to get Jesus to attempt suicide by jumping off the top of the temple (Luke 4:9–11). Jesus' defense was that He knew Scripture, and He understood the context of Scripture. So He quoted Scripture back to Satan that put it all into the context of what God truly intended to communicate (Luke 4:12).

The devil tried to use Scripture like a spiritual Ouija board, taking it out of context and changing its meaning. Jesus' strategy was to put it back into the context in which God communicated it. He was able to accomplish this because He knew the Scriptures.

WRAPPING UP

Let me summarize what we have been talking about.

God has already communicated much to us through His written Word, the Bible.

In addition to the Bible, God still likes to communicate personally with every one of His children today. We are to listen for God to speak to us. And we must reject anything that contradicts what He said in the Bible.

Finally, we must not try to twist or manipulate Scripture to put words or false promises in God's mouth. And we look to the Holy Spirit to quicken Scripture to us, to recall it to our memory and to speak to us through it.

POINTS TO PONDER

1. What are some types of situations where the Bible gives us clear guidelines and directions about what God wants us to do in that situation?

2. What are some examples of situations in our day-to-day life that the Bible does not address clearly? These are areas where we might need to hear directly from God to discern His will.

3. Has there ever been a time in your life when you, accidentally or intentionally, tried to use a scripture to claim a promise that God had not made to you? How did God go about showing you that you had done this?

FOUR

When You Don't Think You Hear God

God is a communicating God, so He finds many ways to speak to His children. You may think you don't know how to discern God's voice clearly. Nonetheless, God still is actively speaking to you! His desire is for each of us to know and recognize His voice clearly and accurately. But He has many ways by which He speaks to us, even before we know how to hear Him clearly.

These are just a few of the ways God speaks to us and leads us:

- Object lessons
- Repetition
- Everyday life
- Divine coincidences
- Internal promptings
- Checks in our spirit
- Conviction of the Holy Spirit

- Hearing someone share something and getting an inner witness
- Through a book, teaching, movie or song
- Through dreams

You have no doubt experienced the Lord communicating with you in some of these ways. I am going to share examples of each, and my guess is that you will relate to one or more of them. You will see that God has been communicating with you and leading you all along! God is a loving Father who delights in being involved in many details of our lives. He has a way of leading us even when we don't realize that He is doing it. See how many of the following you have experienced.

OBJECT LESSONS

An *object lesson* is when God uses something in the natural to illustrate a spiritual principle. Jesus used a lot of object lessons when He taught. For instance, He said that faith is like a mustard seed—the tiniest of seeds—that grows into a huge tree where the birds of the air can rest in its shade (Mark 4:31–32). The mustard seed is a truth from everyday life. The corresponding spiritual truth, quickened to us through the Holy Spirit, is that even the smallest faith, when exercised, will grow into something spectacular and solid as we see God's faithfulness come through for us. Mark 4:33 tells us that "with many such parables He [Jesus] spoke the word to them as they were able to hear it."

Sometimes the object lessons God teaches us are simple, and at other times they are profound.

God loves to use object lessons to which we can relate, ones that speak directly to us from our everyday experiences. Ed and I do not have children, but we have two dogs, Lucky and Salsa. We love these dogs dearly; they are almost like kids to us. God frequently speaks to me from incidents with the dogs. Let me share one story with you.

One morning I got out of bed and went downstairs to the kitchen for a drink. When heading back upstairs, I noticed that Lucky, one of my two dogs, had placed himself squarely at the head of the stairs—lying down and looking at me expectantly with those big brown eyes of his as I headed up the stairs toward him. Now anyone who owns and loves dogs knows that look. It means, "Pet me! Love me!"

Lucky is a big dog (a 110-pound German Shepherd) and was pretty effectively blocking my path. I would not be able to get past him without stepping over him. I bent down and gave him a good pet, rubbed his tummy and kissed his forehead. As I did so, I could hear the thump of my other dog's tail wagging. She was still lying on her bed, located on the landing at the top of our staircase. I knew she wanted to be petted, too. I finished petting Lucky, and then I went over to pet and love my other dog.

Quite unexpectedly, the Lord spoke to me. "Teresa, why did you pet Lucky before you petted Salsa? Do you love him more than you love her?"

"No, Lord, of course not. I love both my dogs the same."

"Then why did you pet Lucky first?" He asked.

"Because Lucky had planted himself in my path. Therefore I ran into him first."

"Exactly," the Lord said. "He watched where you had gone and predicted where you would be going. He placed himself in your path. Meanwhile Salsa just stayed where she was in her bed. So, to which one did you give your attention first? You gave it to the one who planted himself in the middle of your path.

"It's like that with Me and My children, too," God continued. "I love them all equally, but the ones I will deal with and minister to first are those who watch where I am going and place themselves in My path. I will meet the ones who just stay where they are, waiting for Me. But first I will meet those who go out of their way to seek Me. So, Teresa, continue to watch where I am going. Continue to plant yourself in the middle of My path, and I will continue to meet you there."

When we hear the Lord's voice speaking distinctively into our thoughts, the revelation is not always dramatic. Sometimes the quickening of the Holy Spirit feels more like we have suddenly realized something. This happened to me recently while I was speaking at a conference. The worship time had just finished, and it was my turn to welcome the people to the meeting. The microphone went dead just as the last song ended. I came up to take the microphone, and nothing happened.

This particular meeting was attended by only about two hundred people, so I put the microphone down and began to project my voice. I practically had to shout, but at least everyone could hear me. After a few minutes, someone behind me tapped me on the shoulder and handed me a microphone. Apparently the sound system had been repaired.

I took it and whispered, "Can you hear me?" My voice filled the room, and everyone nodded.

The contrast was stark. My gentle whisper rang more clearly through the room when amplified by the sound system than when I had been projecting as much as I could on my own. It was so easy to whisper into the microphone, much easier than when I'd shouted on my own. The spiritual analogy hit me in an instant. I suddenly realized that trying to walk the Christian walk in our own strength is similar to trying to speak to a crowd without a microphone. Our best efforts may seem to get by for a season, but it is so much easier and more effective to let the Holy Spirit help us—just as the sound system helped me address the people.

We need to lean on God instead of on our own abilities. I shared my revelation with the two hundred conference attendees, explaining how God had "set up this incident" to illustrate how much easier and more powerful it is when we lean on the Holy Spirit instead of on our natural ability. God had used an example from everyday life to communicate a spiritual truth to us.

REPETITION

Repetition is running into the same thing over and over again until it finally dawns on us that God is trying to tell us something. Sometimes it is precisely the same thing over and over. Other times it is similar or related things. As we hear, see, feel or experience something over and over again, it dawns on us that these repetitions are more than mere coincidence—*God is communicating with us.*

Perhaps one morning you wake up with a prayer burden. Later as you read your Bible, a verse jumps out at you, addressing what you were praying about. When you turn on the radio, a song comes on that contains phrases from the portion of Scripture you read earlier. When you chat with a friend, she says, "God really showed me something the other day from…," quoting the same scripture that grabbed you that morning. Still later, when you sit down in church, the Bible on the pew next to you lies open to that same verse. Every time you turn around,

39

there is that verse again. You begin to wonder if God is trying to tell you something—and He probably is. The Lord loves to use repetition to get our attention.

One time God wanted me to spend a month fasting and praying for Israel. I was not particularly keen to do that, so I tried to ignore the conviction of the Holy Spirit within my heart. Every time I opened my Bible, I saw scriptures like Luke 2:37 about a woman "who did not depart from the temple, but served God with fastings and prayers night and day." Or I'd see verses like Psalm 122:6, which says, "Pray for the peace of Jerusalem." So I put my Bible down and turned on the television. All the programs had something to do with Israel.

One station had a documentary about the history of Israel. Another station was showing the movie *Raid on Entebbe*, where Israeli special forces rescue Jewish victims of a hijacking. So I turned to the health channel—and they were doing a documentary on the medical benefits of fasting! Feeling frustrated, I turned off the television and went to a secular social event. Everyone I met there seemed to be either Jewish or had recently visited Israel!

No matter where I turned, I could not get away from it. Everything I ran into either had to do with fasting or had to do with Israel. So I went home and called a friend. All she could talk about was how God was putting it on her heart to fast. It was very clear to me that God was trying to tell me something. I did not want to listen because I did not relish the idea of a thirty-day fast. But God had a way of using repetition to make His wishes very clear. (I finally did give in and do the fast, and it was a very powerful experience for me.)

EVERYDAY LIFE

God tends to show up and speak to us from our everyday life experiences. One day as we go about our daily routine, suddenly He breaks in and gives us a revelation from them. These can be fairly simple, or they can be incredibly deep. They can broaden our understanding of God's nature, or they can be a directive.

God will use your everyday life experiences to communicate to you. Perhaps as you begin your spring cleaning, you will be cleaning out your closets and getting rid of the old stuff you no longer need. While you work the Lord may begin to speak to you about a spiritual housecleaning, convicting you about getting rid of things—attitudes, practices and such—that you have been hanging onto. These things may be holding you back in your walk with Him. God uses natural day-to-day life experiences to launch into spiritual issues.

Perhaps you have an unappreciative teenager. Even when your teen ignores you, or lets you down, you continue to make time for that child. You remain faithful to and supportive of your teen. Even when he doesn't seem to want you around, you make yourself available to him. Yet the more you reach out to him, the more your teen seems to take you for granted. It hurts, but you do not love your son (or daughter) any less.

Perhaps in the midst of this difficult and ongoing situation, God gives you a revelation of His faithfulness. You realize He is also faithful to those who take Him for granted and won't receive the help He tries to give them. You have an understanding of the pain it must cause God's heart and of His ability to keep on loving them. God has spoken to you in your life experiences, enabling you to understand one aspect of His nature better.

DIVINE COINCIDENCES

A *divine coincidence* is a moment when events or circumstances fall together in such a way that the hand of God is evident in your circumstances. As you sit back and look, you can see that God has been orchestrating events to lead you into the center of His perfect will. Sometimes this can be fairly simple, and sometimes it can be quite elaborate. Sometimes, as the events are unfolding, the leading of God is very clear. At other times His plans may seem very elusive and unclear until they have been accomplished.

Let me illustrate with a story that a pastor from Cleveland shared at a conference. He was in the midst of putting together a book on the spiritual heritage of the greater-Cleveland area. He had been praying for the Lord to give him revelation along these lines. One day he took his car to the repair shop for routine maintenance. He dropped the car off, talked with the mechanic, who was named Milan, and returned home.

Later he called to see if the car was ready, and inadvertently dialed the wrong number. When someone answered, he asked, "Is this Milan?"

The person replied, "No, Milan is another twenty minutes down the road from here." Then that person hung up. The pastor thought that was odd, and then realized he had misdialed. But he had discovered that there was a place called *Milan* not far from where he lived. He redialed, got the mechanic and learned that his car was ready.

On his way to pick up his car, the car in which he was riding stopped at a traffic light. The car in front of them had a bumper sticker on it: *Milan, Ohio.*

The pastor began to wonder if God was trying to tell

him something about Milan. In a few short hours, he had met a mechanic by that name, discovered a city by that name was located close to home and saw a bumper sticker for Milan.

After he picked up his car, he drove to the city of Milan. When he got there, he encountered someone who told him the story of how the city had been founded as a Christian community. He learned about an old library containing papers from the city's founding fathers. When he went to the library, he found several important documents that helped him with the research he was doing on that geographical area.

God had used the coincidences about Milan to get him to that city. Once there, he discovered a little, out-of-the-way library that contained documents vitally important to the research he was doing.

INTERNAL PROMPTINGS

Internal promptings are strong urges to do—or not do—something. You can't explain why you feel that way, but it is in you. Sometimes the intensity inside just keeps building until you do it. At other times you just happen to do something that turns out to be precisely the right thing for you to do. You cannot explain why you did it, but somehow you knew to do it.

The Holy Spirit frequently leads us this way. Many times we do not realize that God is speaking, and we are responding. We may think we are being intuitive, or we may think it is just a coincidence.

Let me share a simple example. One time I was part of a leadership team that was having a potluck team meeting. I had already purchased something for the potluck, but as I was driving to our meeting, I noticed a bakery I had never seen before. I felt strongly impressed to stop at the bakery and check it out. I was running a few minutes late, but the urge was so strong I stopped anyway.

Once inside the store, I "just knew" I had to get a German chocolate cake. I didn't know why, but I just knew it. I bought the cake and took it to the potluck.

The event was being held in the back yard, so I let myself in through the side gate. As I rounded the curve to where the people were, they had just begun singing "Happy Birthday." It turned out that it was the pastor's wife's birthday. She had kept it a secret, but it had slipped out just moments before I arrived.

As I walked up, carrying a cake box, I chirped in, "Well, I brought the birthday cake."

"I will know it was the Lord," the birthday woman replied, "if it is a German chocolate cake. We had a family tradition when I was growing up. Every year for my birthday, my mother would bake me a German chocolate cake."

I opened the box and showed everyone the German chocolate cake. The pastor's wife was so excited and blessed that God had provided her with the traditional birthday cake!

Here is another example. I was someone's house guest during a ministry trip. I arrived after the evening service. The wife wanted to make me a snack, so she sent her husband to the corner market for a specific item. I was hungry and did want a snack, but what I really wanted was my favorite...Ritz crackers. Being polite, I did not mention it to them. He came back ten minutes later with two items in tow—the requested snack and a box of Ritz crackers.

The wife asked why he got the crackers, since they

never eat them. He had no idea why; he saw them and it "felt right," so he bought them. Then I explained that this was the Lord prompting him. I wanted Ritz crackers, and the Lord knew it.

Look back on those times where you just happened to be in the right place at the right time. Think about other times when you felt prompted to do the right thing. You may have been led by the Holy Spirit. You followed His directions and did His will without even realizing it!

A CHECK IN OUR SPIRIT

Sometimes the Lord gives us a *check in our spirit.* It is as if an internal alarm goes off, and suddenly we feel leery or cautious about something. We don't have any reason in the natural to feel this way, but we feel this way nonetheless. It may be in regard to an activity; we don't do it because we feel it is not safe. It may be in regard to a person; we feel the person's motives are not what they seem to be. It may be in regard to a teaching; it simply does not feel right, although you cannot put your finger on why.

When we get a check in our spirit, we tend to slow down, look into things more carefully and pray more for God's direction and a revelation of His will. A check in the spirit may cause us to delay making a decision, or it may drive us to search the Scriptures regarding something. We may even feel led to fast and pray for clarity and God's direction. Sometimes the Lord will give us a check in our spirit to keep us from being misled or taken advantage of. Sometimes the checks in our spirit are for our protection, to keep us from physical danger.

A check in the spirit does not mean that we will necessarily avoid the person or situation about which we feel the check. Rather, it may cause us to move more slowly, to pray and research and check things out. One time I was working with a travel agent to purchase some airline tickets. The agent seemed nice enough, and the deal sounded good. But I had a check in my spirit about it, so I delayed purchasing the tickets for a day. The next day the tickets went on sale for 35 percent off the purchase price originally quoted to me. The Lord had given me a check about the situation, and it caused me to slow down. Once I slowed down, I ended up being able to take advantage of a very good deal that was not available when I originally planned to purchase the tickets.

The Lord may give you a check about a person who wants to do what seems to be a favor for you. Or He may give you a check about an activity in which you want to become involved. Perhaps you are driving down the freeway, going precisely the speed limit, and suddenly you feel a check in your spirit and slow down. As you round a bend in the road, you see that traffic is at a complete standstill. If you had not slowed down, you would have piled into the stopped cars.

Checks in our spirit are one of God's ways of protecting us. The main purpose is to cause us to slow down and be more cautious. We need time to seek His will proactively in that situation or interaction.

Sometimes we disregard the checks in our spirit because they seem "counter-intuitive." Many times when we later look back on that situation, we find ourselves saying, "I had a bad feeling about that. I should have paid attention to that check in my spirit about it."

CONVICTION OF THE HOLY SPIRIT

If you are a child of the King, there are times when the

Holy Spirit *convicts you.* This goes with the territory, and I am sure you have experienced it. Perhaps you were involved in an activity or action, and the Lord let you know it displeased Him. Suddenly you had a strong sense that it was wrong and that the Lord would not approve. Perhaps you felt dirty and knew that the Holy Spirit was convicting you. Or you may have sensed the Lord's sadness at your behavior.

Sometimes conviction works in the other direction. You may be resisting something God wants you to do, and the Holy Spirit is convicting your spirit about it. Maybe you brushed off a beggar who asked for money. Suddenly you remember the verse that says, "Give to those who ask you." You have a strong sense that you should have given the beggar something. You think to yourself, *Next time I will give.* You may wonder if you should go back and find that person and hand him some money.

God may be convicting you to spend some time with a lonely person who is in great need of love. Because you do not particularly like this person, you resist doing it. It is not a pleasant task, but the conviction of the Lord comes on you to do so. It surfaces over and over, making you uncomfortable. You become aware that you are resisting God.

These are examples of the conviction of the Holy Spirit. There are many different ways that the Holy Spirit convicts those who belong to Jesus. He does this to help us get right with God—not to make us feel bad.

GETTING AN INNER WITNESS AS SOMEONE SHARES SOMETHING

Did you know that sometimes God speaks to us through other people? There will be times when your spirit grabs hold of a truth as someone speaks to you. Something inside sparks, and you just know that what is being said is right. This is called an inner witness. The Holy Spirit gives us an *inner witness* when He wants to confirm or underscore something.

At times you will need advice about a situation you are facing. You may go to several people for advice, and each one tells you something different. But something one person says clicks with you, as if God Himself were speaking it to you.

Down in the depths of your being, you know that what you just heard is correct. Part of a sermon or teaching may seem to "hit the nail on the head" with you, speaking directly to your heart.

God uses others to speak to you at times. He quickens what they say to your spirit to get your attention and to let you know the truths came from Him to you.

GOD SPEAKS THROUGH BOOKS, TEACHINGS, MOVIES OR SONGS

God is not at all limited in the ways that He can speak to us. He uses so many things. God tends to speak to me through old war movies. I never thought I would like that sort of movie. But a while ago, I watched one. To my surprise I liked it, and I began to watch others. When the movie portrayed the courage and dedication of the soldiers, God began to speak to my heart about those topics. One movie portrayed a soldier laying down his life to save his platoon by jumping on a grenade and covering it with his body. God began to speak to me about preferring one another, about laying down our lives for each other, about love and caring in the body of Christ.

God has spoken to me through songs many times.

One time I was going about my day-to-day business, sort of caught up in the routine. Suddenly the words to an old song began running through my mind. Over and over again I heard the chorus, which talked about rejoicing and being glad in each day. It suddenly dawned on me that God wanted me to rejoice in my day-to-day walk with Him. He wanted my joy to be full. Through that song, God had spoken to me. Now He had my attention, and I began to press into Him. As I did that, He began to fill me with His joy. I ended up bubbling over with His joy the entire day.

God likes to do that. He is a very creative God, and He likes to be highly creative by using various commonplace things to communicate with us.

DREAMS

Sometimes God speaks to us in dreams. The Bible is full of examples of God-sent dreams. The wise men were warned in a dream to avoid Herod and go home another way (Matt. 2:12). While returning from Egypt, Joseph was warned in a dream to take his family to Galilee instead of back to Judah (Matt. 2:22).

We know that God speaks to believers and unbelievers alike in dreams. God spoke to Abimelech (a heathen king) in a dream, advising him to return Abraham's wife, Sarah, to him (Gen. 20:3). In Egypt, Pharaoh had a dream about seven years of plenty followed by seven years of famine (Gen. 41:1–8). He acted on that dream and built up grain storehouses, enabling him to feed his people when the famine hit.

God speaks to some people in their dreams quite frequently. For others, this is a rare occurrence. God has only spoken to me in dreams a few times. One time I was seeking Him for direction about whether or not to go on a missions trip to India, and He answered me by a dream. Another time God warned me in a dream that a ministry partner was going to break away and do his own thing. When it happened, I was neither surprised nor devastated.

I know people to whom God frequently and constantly speaks in dreams. I know others who think they never dream and are not aware of any time in their lives when God spoke to them through a dream. However, most believers will have occasional dreams from God during which the Lord communicates to them understanding, direction or revelation.

Dreams can be symbolic, or they can be very distinct. My dream about going on the missions trip to India was symbolic. Typically I am not one to remember my dreams, but this one stayed with me. I don't know how, but I understood the symbolism in the dream and knew what it was communicating to me. On the other hand, the dream warning me about my ministry partner who was breaking away to start a ministry was not symbolic at all. It was clear and distinct. And that is exactly what happened shortly after I had the dream. It was easy to bless my partner and let him go because God had spoken to me about it through a dream.

WRAP UP

God uses many different ways to communicate with us and to guide us. I have shared some of these ways in this chapter so that you can hear God and respond to Him, even before you have learned to discern His voice clearly. God will continue to speak to you in these ways.

But He wants to invite you into a more specific, more detailed level of communication. He wants to speak to you clearly and directly. He wants you to learn to recognize His voice and to be able to dialogue with Him about the events in your life. There is much He desires to tell you directly. The next few chapters will explain how to fine-tune your hearing so that He can speak more clearly and more distinctly to you.

POINTS TO PONDER

1. Share an example of a time when God communicated to you using one of the methods described in this chapter. Which time stands out the most in your memory? Describe the details of that communication from God.

2. Which communication method did you identify with the most strongly? Which was the hardest to relate to?

3. Does God use a wide variety of methods to communicate with you, or does He stick to only a few?

4. Were you aware that it was God communicating to you, or did you realize it later as you looked back on the experience?

5. Have you ever felt an inner witness or confirmation from the Holy Spirit? Can you describe what it feels like or how you knew it was the Holy Spirit? How can you tell that from your own feelings on the matter?

FIVE

Three Voices That Try to Speak to Us

We all want to hear God's voice and recognize when He is speaking to us. That is a good goal, and it is not difficult. But we need to be aware there are also two other voices that may try to get in on the action. Before we open ourselves up to hearing God, we want to understand all three voices and learn how to distinguish between them. Once we are able to recognize how other voices may try to imitate God's voice, it becomes easier to recognize His voice.

VOICE 1—GOD'S VOICE

God's voice is the most important voice to hear. Sometimes His voice will be very distinct and easy to recognize. But sometimes it may sound very similar to your own thoughts. His voice may come in other forms. For instance, there have been times when I thought my mind was wandering, but it was really God speaking to me and directing my thinking. There have been times when God spoke to me by recalling things to my memory. Sometimes it was a Bible verse that seemed to address an issue I was facing. At other times I have remembered something someone had said to me that fit my current situation. Sometimes an item I read days (or weeks or months) earlier came to mind and applied to my current circumstances. Each of these examples shows that God was getting my attention to communicate with me.

God communicates with us in various ways. He may speak conversationally. He may show us pictures and images. He may speak to us through senses and impressions. Or we may find that suddenly we know some information we did not previously know, as if the Holy Spirit just downloaded it into our spirits. In other words, we may *hear* Him. We may *see* what He shows us, or we may *sense* or *just know* what He is communicating. God will not usually limit Himself to just one of these ways when He talks to you. However, He may have a strong preference for one method and use it more than He uses the others in His communication with you.

When God speaks to us conversationally, it is usually in our thoughts. In fact, God's voice may sound so much like our own thoughts that we fail to realize it is God—and not "just me." In this case, our big struggle will be, "Was that *God*, or was that *just my imagination?*" To tell the two apart requires getting to know your own imagination—and to know God's voice better.

We can recognize our own thoughts and desires. And by spending time in intimacy with God, we can get to know Him better than we know our own imagination. We get to know God through worship, prayer and meditation. We learn His ways and discover His character by reading, studying and memorizing His Word. The more we know *what we are like*, and the more we know *what He is like*, the easier it is to tell His voice from our imagination when we hear Him speak to us in His still, small voice.

Sometimes He may give us a picture or image in our mind's eye. Usually when this happens, we know immediately that it is from God. But we are often confused about "What does it mean?" or "What is God trying to say?" If God speaks to us pictorially, we may need to ask Him to help us understand what He desires to communicate. If we press in and ask God about what we have seen, He will usually give us more clarification. He may do this by changing the image or zooming in to focus on something in particular or panning back to give you a bigger picture and broader context. Or He may choose another mechanism of communication to explain the picture to you.

Amos had such an experience. God showed him a basket of fruit, and then God talked with him about what it meant (Amos 8:1–6). When God gives you a spiritual picture, learn to ask Him to explain what He is showing to you. Ask Him why He is showing it to you and what He would like you to do in response.

Sometimes God gives us an impression, something we "just know" even though we can't explain why or how we know. This type of communication closely resembles human intuition, and we may question, "Is that God, or is it just my own intuition?" When we get a *hunch* from God, we may be tempted to discount it and lean on our own understanding of the situation instead. We may have to fight our own reasoning, which will try to talk us out of believing what God just communicated. When this happens, we have to slow down and look at our impressions, bring them back to God and ask Him, "Lord, is this You?"

VOICE 2—OUR OWN HEART

The ways that our own heart speaks to us are as diverse as people are diverse. Many of us tend to be very hard and critical of ourselves. Therefore, sometimes we think God is saying something negative or harsh to us when it is really our own hearts that are condemning us. The Holy Spirit will *convict* us, but He won't *condemn* us (Rom. 8:1). Conviction moves us to change our behavior that separates us from God and draws us close to Him. Condemnation just makes us feel bad and hopeless and tends to push us away from God.

Others of us are very undisciplined and lax with ourselves. If we lack spiritual discipline and control, sometimes our hearts may tell us to "take it easy on yourself"—and we will think it is advice straight from God. We can detect our error with this quickly, because we know that God's voice never violates Scripture. Therefore, if the voice we hear is telling us it is OK to indulge in a sin, we can know for certain that it is not God's voice.

We need to know what our common "errors" and thought patterns are. Then we will know when to be suspicious of something we hear and to double-check it with God before we act upon it. The better we know the Bible, the easier it is to discern when something we have heard does not line up with Scripture. Knowing God's Word is an absolute criterion for us, isn't it? God is not a liar, and He does not change. If He said it in His Word, He is not going to contradict it when speaking directly to us.

You have heard people say that it is harder to hear God clearly when you are emotionally involved. Do you know why they say that? Because the more you have at stake, the more your own heart is likely to jump in with opinions, imitating God's voice. Many divorced people have told me they heard God promise that He would restore their marriages. They held on to that promise for months or years, only to find that their ex-spouse became engaged—or married—to someone else. There is no doubt that they heard "someone" tell them the marriage would be restored. But the key question is, Was it really God, or did their own heart tell them what they yearned to hear?

Always be careful to double-check your hearing in areas where you are emotionally involved. Those are the areas where your own heart is most likely to deceive you.

There are other times when your hearing of God's voice degrades. At these times you are more likely to hear your own heart on a matter and think it is God. The most common time is when you are tired or exhausted. So what do you do about it? That one is easy…rest. There have been times where I have come to God exhausted yet desperate to hear from Him. Instead of talking to me right away, He usually puts me to sleep so I can rest. Once I am rested and fresh, I am able to hear Him more easily.

Another time when it is hard to hear God is when you are not walking in His peace in some area of your life. When your mind is racing, or when you are upset or anxious, you may not be able to hear God clearly.

We may have "problem areas" where it is harder to discern God's voice from our own hearts. People who have a prolonged history of financial difficulties often find it hard to hear God in the area of finances. They may hear Him just fine in all other matters, but when it comes to finances, their own hearts jump in and confuse the issue. For myself, there is a relationship about which I simply cannot hear God. I had a "best friend" with whom I had become very close. My friend had a lot of wonderful traits, but she was sometimes manipulative and controlling. I had given her my heart and loved her dearly in the Lord. If I would not do what she wanted, she would become extremely coercive or withdraw her friendship and approval to try to force me to do things her way.

I did not know how to handle the way she treated me. I would go to God and ask Him about her. My hearing in regard to my friend was totally messed up—my own heart was too engaged. I was unable to sort out when it was God and when it was my own heart speaking. I learned that I must not trust my hearing on the topic of this friendship. I can hear fine in most other situations, but I suspect anything that I think God is saying to me about my friend.

Both of these areas—finances and friendships—are examples of areas where we may find it hard to hear God clearly when He speaks to us because our own heart or mind is so engaged.

Finally, if sin or unforgiveness is separating you from God, this can also interfere with your ability to hear Him clearly. The best strategy for that problem is to get right with God—then you can get on with hearing Him more clearly.

VOICE 3—THE ENEMY'S VOICE

The enemy can try to imitate God's voice to us. The enemy's imitation may even be more confusing than our own heart or mind's imitation of God's voice. For instance, he may quote Scripture to us, as he did in the temptations of Jesus (Luke 4:10–11). Satan quoted Scripture to Jesus, and it sounded rather convincing. However, Satan twisted the context and meaning of those verses, trying to lead Jesus astray. Jesus was not taken in by this because He knew the Scriptures well—and because He knew the Father well.

Satan will try to do the same with us. Fortunately, the Lord has given us authority over the enemy, and we have the Holy Spirit residing in us so that we may not be deceived.

The more we have prepared ourselves by knowing God and knowing His Word, the less easily we are taken in by the enemy's deceptions and imitation of God's Word. But the enemy can even use our knowledge—or lack of it—about God's Word against us. He can whisper to us, "You don't know the Bible well enough to trust yourself to hear God's voice." If we listen to that, we will never feel qualified enough to discern God's voice. In that case, we will never start listening to Him.

We can trust that when we are sincerely seeking God on His terms, He is not going to allow us to fall into (and remain in) deception. Matthew 7:7–11 gives us a scriptural precedence for understanding this. It says:

> Ask and it will be given to you; seek and you will find; knock and the door will be opened to you. For everyone who asks receives; he who seeks finds; and to him who knocks, the door will be opened.
>
> Which of you, if his son asks for bread, will give him a stone? Or if he asks for a fish, will give him a snake? If you, then, though you are evil,

know how to give good gifts to your children,
how much more will your Father in heaven give
good gifts to those who ask him!

—NIV

When we ask God for good things, He will not give
us something hurtful or dangerous. God is not going
to give us wicked things when we ask Him for good
things. So if we ask Him to speak to us, He will not let
a demon speak to us instead.

God has given us authority over all the power of the
enemy (Luke 10:19). Even the demons have to obey us
(Luke 10:17). When we are first learning to discern
God's voice, it can be helpful to take authority in Jesus'
name and forbid the enemy to interfere or imitate God's
voice. I do that when I teach classes or do exercises in
workshops. I first lead the group through a prayer of
faith and positive confession; then I lead them through
an authority prayer, forbidding enemy interference.
This type of prayer can be quite helpful, especially for
those who are still learning to discern what God's voice
sounds like.

There is one specific circumstance about which we
need to give some clarification. There will be some people over whom the enemy has been granted a degree of
authority. The most common case is people who are suf-
fering from demonic oppression because of some past
activity that invited demonic spirits in, usually (but not
always) before they were saved. That activity gave the
enemy a "legal right" over an area of the person's life.

An example of such activities would be New Age
involvement or involvement in psychic practices before
salvation. For these people, the enemy has a legitimate
claim to exercise control or heavy influence over a

portion of their thinking or behavior. When such a person tries to take authority over the enemy, Satan seems to be exempt from having to obey that person. Authority prayers preventing enemy interference do not seem to be very effective with these individuals.

Another example along these lines is the individual whom God the Father has delivered over to the tormentors (demons) because of unforgiveness in that person's heart. (See Matthew 18:32–35.) If you fall into this category, you need to deal with the enemy stronghold over your life. After it is dealt with, the enemy won't have the authority to hinder you in hearing your loving heavenly Father speak to you.

If that stronghold is caused by a past dedication to evil or evil behavior, renounce it and proclaim your allegiance only to the lordship of Jesus in your life. If the stronghold is caused by sin, turn from the sin, repent and stop doing it. If the stronghold is caused by unforgiveness or bitterness, choose, as an act of your will, to forgive (because you know that pleases your heavenly Father) and begin to release forgiveness. If the enemy oppression is too strong for you to deal with on your own, get help. If you need deliverance, then get deliverance. If you need someone to walk alongside of you to support you and help keep you accountable, find someone. (Your pastor or a leader or elder in your church is often a good place to begin.) In short, if the enemy has a "legal right" to interfere with your ability to hear God, then deal with that legal right and get it taken away.

If the enemy does not have a legal right to interfere, then he is not going to be a big or long-term factor keeping you from hearing God. Take precautions when you are first starting out—pray authority prayers to forbid him to interfere. Review your heart with the

Holy Spirit, and make sure it is right with God. Then trust your heavenly Father to give you good gifts (just as He said He would) instead of evil ones. Trust Him to give you His voice and not a demon's voice when you are sincerely seeking to hear Him and are committed to obeying Him once you have heard Him.

POINTS TO PONDER

1. What area of your own heart is most likely to imitate God's voice to you?

2. Have you ever experienced a time when the enemy came in with lies of condemnation and rejection or tried to speak to you in some other way? How did you discern that it was the enemy's voice and not God's voice or your own heart? What scriptures are most helpful in combating the area where the enemy tries to speak to you?

3. How do you think you will go about recognizing God's voice from the other two voices (from your own heart and from the enemy's voice)? Are there times when it is difficult for you to tell them apart? Is there an area in your walk with God where you need to get to know Him better so that you can discern His voice more easily from the other voices?

SIX

Positioning Ourselves to Hear God's Voice

In the business world, the term *positioning* refers to the practice of observing what is needed, fulfilling any prerequisites and being in the right place. Positioning assures you that when an opportunity comes along, you can seize it. The reason you can seize the opportunity is twofold: First, you have prepared yourself, and second, you have demonstrated motivation by being in the right place and watching expectantly.

My dogs are not in the business world, but they certainly understand the concept of positioning themselves. They practice it every time we sit down to eat a meal at our kitchen table. From wherever they were in the house, the dogs appear magically on the floor by the table, in a position where they can make eye contact with us. Then they watch us expectantly. If you have dogs, I am sure you know what I mean. Apparently one of the "golden rules of doggies" is, "Be present and easily accessible whenever humans are eating, because one of the humans may desire to share some food with you."

Positioning is preparing ourselves and being in the right place at the right time. There are two areas in the Spirit where we need to position ourselves to more effectively hear God. To hear God's voice clearly, we need to develop an intimate relationship with Him. And we need to commit firmly in our heart and spirit to His lordship in our life, obeying Him in all things.

The more intimate your relationship is with another person, the easier it is to recognize that person's voice above all others. Have you ever telephoned a close friend, listened to that person say "hello," and responded with "Hi..."? Then before you can get another word out of your mouth, your friend begins, "I am so glad you called! You won't believe what just happened! I am so excited! Let me tell you all about it!" And before you can get another word in, that person is sharing a personal and detailed story with you.

You never told that person who you were. You did not have to, because your friend recognized your voice. In the same way, you recognized that person's voice when they answered the phone. Because you have a mutual friendship and a close relationship with each other, you immediately recognize each other's voice.

On the other hand, if you telephone someone you hardly know, you will probably begin the conversation by asking if you have the right person and identifying who you are. You do not know that person's voice. You do not expect that person to recognize your voice because you do not yet share a close relationship.

Our ability to recognize each other's voice is directly tied to the depth of our relationship together.

It works like that in the spirit, too. The closer and more intimate our relationship is with God, the easier it becomes to recognize His voice when He speaks to us. We discover He speaks to us frequently and that He has much to say to us.

When Jesus was on the earth, He developed this concept in His teachings. He often talked about God and man "knowing" each other personally. He talked about the tie between intimacy with God and hearing God's voice. Let's look at an example in John 10:27. Jesus said, "My sheep hear My voice, and I know them, and they follow Me."

This verse tells us that Jesus expects us to hear and recognize His voice. He expects us to follow Him. But did you catch the middle phrase? It says, "… and I know them." With those words, Jesus ties an intimate relationship to Him with our ability to hear His voice.

Let's look back a few verses at John 10:11–15.

> I am the good shepherd. The good shepherd gives His life for the sheep. But a hireling, he who is not the shepherd, one who does not own the sheep, sees the wolf coming and leaves the sheep and flees; and the wolf catches the sheep and scatters them. The hireling flees because he is a hireling and does not care about the sheep. I am the good shepherd; and I know My sheep, and am known by My own. As the Father knows Me, even so I know the Father; and I lay down my life for the sheep.

Jesus is talking about intimacy between God and man in this passage. He starts and ends by showing His commitment to us. He says that a good shepherd is willing to lay down his life to protect his flock. We know that He is drawing a parallel between things of the natural (shepherds and sheep) and things of the Spirit (God's relationship to His creation).

Jesus did, in fact, lay down His life for us. Our sins had separated us from God. But Jesus was fully committed to make it possible for mankind to enter into intimate and personal relationship with God, so He became the atonement for our sins. This is the Good News of the gospel, isn't it? Jesus Himself died for our sins and rose again so that we are no longer separated from our Creator. His sacrifice is what makes it possible for us to enter into a close personal relationship with God.

In His example, Jesus mentions two other forces that are at work—the hireling and the wolf. *Hirelings* are those who serve God out of their own agendas and purposes. They usually try to make us become dependent on them instead of on God. They do not help us grow in God or develop a deep relationship with Him. They don't "hold up" under pressure. We cannot depend on them. When it becomes "costly," they are no longer interested in helping us. They let us down and even disillusion some people. God's solution for this problem is to advise us to get to know the true Shepherd instead of putting our faith in men and hirelings.

The *wolf* represents Satan, who wants to scatter us or keep us from living in intimacy and right relationship with God. Even while Jesus is at work in our lives, inviting us into closer intimacy with God, Satan is at work in our lives trying to drive a wedge between God and ourselves. He is trying to separate or scatter us from God.

It remains God's desire for each of us to be in a deep and personal relationship with Him. Verses 14 and 15 talk about this intimacy, the knowing and being known. Not only does Jesus know each of us intimately, but He also expects us to know Him intimately as well. This all ties in with verse 27, which says, "My sheep hear My voice, and I know them." Jesus gives us a clear tie between a deep personal relationship with God and our ability to clearly hear and discern His voice.

In John 15:15, Jesus emphasized this intimate relationship again by saying:

> No longer do I call you servants, for a servant does not know what his master is doing; but I have called you friends, for all things that I heard from My Father I have made known to you.

In short, as we draw into friendship with God, He reveals more of Himself to us. We get to know Him better, so it becomes easier to recognize His voice. We can understand this principle from our relationships in the natural. When we know someone well, we know that person's likes and dislikes; we know the character of that person. We know what that person would or would not be likely to say. We have spent time with that person, and we recognize the very sound of that person's voice. The same thing holds in our walk with God. The more time we spend with Him, the easier it is to recognize Him.

It is wonderful to know God, to be in deep intimacy with Him and to be able to clearly hear and discern His voice!

Yet, there can be a downside to knowing God's voice. The more clearly you can hear Him, the more accountable He holds you to obey what He says to you. In other words, you will get in more trouble for disobeying God when you can hear His voice clearly than if you don't understand what it is that He wants you to do.

Jesus tells us over and over that He expects to be obeyed. (See John 14:15, 21; 15:14 and many other verses.) Jesus expects obedience, and He expects it to flow out of our great love for Him and out of our intimate relationship with Him. He expects us to love Him. He expects us to demonstrate that love by obeying Him, by doing what He tells us to do.

Jesus didn't mince words when He told us that as our ability to hear God increases, so does our accountability to obey what He says. Look at Luke 12:47–48:

> And that servant who knew his master's will, and did not prepare himself or do according to his will, shall be beaten with many stripes. But he who did not know, yet committed things deserving of stripes, shall be beaten with few. For everyone to whom much is given, from him much will be required; and to whom much has been committed, of him they will ask the more.

What do these verses mean to us in the context of hearing God's voice? If we want to learn to hear God's voice more clearly, we had better be fully committed to obeying Him when He does speak to us. We will not get the option of saying, "I don't like that, Lord; I am going to ignore what You said." God is quite serious about this commitment to obedience. He won't teach us to hear His voice if we have no intention of listening to Him. This is actually a kindness on God's part, since we are held at a higher level of accountability if we hear more clearly.

God knows we need to go through a learning process. Obedience, just like any other aspect of our Christian walk, is something we learn. The good news is that God will become personally involved with us and will help us.

In my case, the Holy Spirit gave me a series of obedience lessons. At first the stakes were fairly low, then they increased. Let me share my experience with you.

One night, early in the process of learning to hear God's voice, I woke up in the wee hours of the morning. I was about to roll over and go back to sleep when the Lord spoke to me very clearly. He said, "Teresa, I want you to go downstairs to your family room and pray." I looked at the clock. It was 2:00 A.M. I tried to roll over and ignore the voice. Then God asked me, "Did you mean it when you asked Me to teach you how to hear My voice?"

"Yes, Lord." I was still groggy, but He had my attention now.

"Then obey Me when I speak to you. Get up, go downstairs to the family room and pray."

So I did. It was cold, so I wrapped myself in a throw blanket. I positioned myself in front of a window, looked out and began to pray for my city. No sooner had I gotten comfortable than God said to me, "OK, now go in the guest bedroom and pray."

"But Lord," I replied, "I've only been praying here for a few minutes!"

"Teresa, I told you to get up and go into the guest bedroom to pray now. Why are you still seated in the family room?"

I got up immediately and went to the guest bedroom. I lay down diagonally across the guest bed and began to pray. A few moments later, I began to doze off. Lying down at 2:15 A.M. was not a smart way to stay awake and pray.

"Teresa," the Lord's voice said. "Get out of the bed and kneel beside it. I don't want you dozing off."

So I did.

I was starting to get really involved in the prayer when, just a few minutes later, God again interrupted my prayer and said, "Now, go to the living room and

68

pray there." Five minutes after that I got a new instruction, "OK, now go in the dining room and pray there." I was beginning to feel frustrated. "Lord," I exclaimed, "I don't get it. You told me to go pray, but You keep interrupting my prayers to bounce me all over the house. Why are You doing this to me?"

"Teresa, I am giving you obedience exercises. You asked Me to teach you My voice. In order for you to learn My voice, you must learn to obey Me when I speak to you. So I am helping you by giving you practice. That is what I am doing right now."

When He said that, it changed my whole perspective on the night's activities. I went from being frustrated to being excited. For the next several nights He woke me up in the wee hours of the morning and bounced me all over the house. I was learning to obey Him. He would tell me what to do, and then I would do it. It was sort of "low-cost obedience," because there was not much at risk in going from room to room to pray.

After a while, and an assortment of simple obedience exercises, God upped the stakes. A friend of mine had recently become engaged to a minister who pastored a small church—so small that the people could not afford to pay him a salary. He lived on faith and did not have money to buy my friend an engagement ring. Even so, my friend told me they had gone window-shopping and had chosen a ring, one that cost more than my own engagement ring.

God spoke to me one evening and said, "Teresa, I want you to give him the money to buy her the ring." God communicated clearly to me what He wanted me to do, and it irked me because it was a lot of money to me. It did not seem fair for me to pay for someone to have a nicer engagement ring than I had myself!

I was faced with a choice: Do I obey God or not? I would be lying if I said it was not a struggle, but I finally chose to obey God. One Saturday evening I took the money to the minister's house and knocked on the door, hoping he would not be home. If he wasn't home, I planned to put the money back into the bank and assume I'd heard wrong after all. But he answered the door. So I explained that God had told me to give him the envelope containing the money, and that it was from God for him to purchase an engagement ring for his fiancée.

He looked astonished, said "thank you" and took the envelope. He did not even invite me into his house—our conversation was over in a matter of minutes. I was obedient but substantially poorer. The door closed, and I started home.

The next day, I heard the story from the pastor's perspective as he shared what had happened in his sermon. He said he had been sitting in his living room, wondering whether or not to call off his engagement. He loved my friend tremendously, but he was not sure it was reasonable to ask her to live on faith as he did. He cried out to God, and God told the pastor to trust Him.

"How can I trust You in this, Lord?" he cried back in anguish. "I can't even afford to buy her an engagement ring. If You won't provide for that, how can I trust You to provide for my wife and family?"

Just then there was a knock at the door, interrupting his prayer. There I was, standing on his doorstep with the envelope. No wonder he looked so astonished! God had used me to answer his prayers, and He spoke deeply to him through the situation.

You see, God does know what He is doing, and He orchestrates incredible circumstances. But He does expect our obedience if we want to be used of Him in

His plans. If we want to hear His voice clearly, we must commit to obey Him—no matter what the cost.

Has my example of costly obedience scared you away from wanting to hear God's voice? I hope not! You can be assured that if you really want to hear and discern God's voice, at least once in the learning process He will hold you to costly obedience—and probably more than once. The price may not always be financial, but it will require you to make a conscious choice to obey Him even though you really don't want to. Hearing His voice clearly carries a big price tag—we must commit to obey what He says to us. Are you still willing?

HEARING HIS VOICE—STEP BY STEP

I am about to give you a step-by-step procedure on how to hear His voice. But before I do, stop and consider whether you are willing to obey Him. I cannot tell you what God will ask you to do, but I can tell you this: If you want to learn to hear His voice, you must be prepared to obey Him no matter what He asks. He may ask you to spend some amount of money above and beyond your regular tithe. He may ask you to change how you spend your leisure time, perhaps to give up a television show or movie that you enjoy. Or He may decide to become involved in your interpersonal relationships, asking you to befriend someone you do not want to befriend. Or He may ask you to give up a relationship He disapproves of.

I can pretty much assure you that at some point in the process, you are going to have a conflict of wills with God. If you want to hear His voice, then you must agree in advance that you will do it *His way* when the conflict occurs. You must commit in your heart and spirit to obey Him once He clearly communicates what He wants you to do.

Please stop for a few minutes, as soon as you finish reading this paragraph, and close your eyes and discuss this with God. Do you desire intimacy with Him? Are you willing for Him to become involved in all areas of your life? Will you commit to obey Him and to give Him lordship of your life? (He will teach you how to walk that out if you are willing.) The Holy Spirit is present with you right now, and He will help you to examine your heart before Him and to begin to cooperate with Him. He is willing to be your teacher and your guide. Please prayerfully consider these questions and commit yourself into His care. He is the most capable teacher there is. (OK, stop now, close your eyes and prayerfully consider these questions before reading on.)

If the answer to these questions is no, you might want to work on the issues of desiring intimacy with God and committing to obey Him before you attempt to proceed any further in learning how to hear God's voice. But if the answer is yes, then please read on. The next several paragraphs will tell you how to begin. There is no time like the present to get started in the wonderful process of learning to hear and recognize God's voice.

PRACTICAL STEPS TO LEARN GOD'S VOICE

Remember that learning God's voice is a process. It takes time. When you learned a new skill or a new sport, you were not very good at it when you began. But over time and with practice, you improved. Eventually you became very proficient at it. This is what will happen for most people as they learn to discern God's voice. It will be a process. You will make mistakes when you first start, but you will become more and more proficient at it over time.

Here are three simple steps to get started in the process. You can start today!

STEP 1—MAKE A COMMITMENT TO THE LORD THAT YOU WANT TO LEARN HIS VOICE.

Decide that you are willing to accept the increased accountability that comes with increased hearing. God will hold you accountable to obey. So make a conscious decision to obey what you hear.

Then ask God to teach you His voice. It really is that simple. You will be entering into a contract with God. Any contract has responsibilities for both sides. Your responsibilities are to seek God, be teachable and commit to obey Him. God's responsibilities are to teach you and to communicate clearly to you in a way you know is from Him, one you can understand. He really will do His part if you will do your part.

God desires to enter into this contract with each of His children. When you enter into it, you are saying, "God, I don't have the wisdom to discern Your voice when You speak to me. So, please give me that wisdom, and teach me to recognize Your voice."

God has already promised to answer that prayer. In James 1:5 we read, "If any of you lacks wisdom, let him ask of God, who gives to all liberally and without reproach, and it will be given to him."

Stop right now to tell God you desire to learn His voice. Tell Him you desire to be teachable. If He will help you to learn, tell Him you will cooperate with Him and obey Him. Then ask God to teach you His voice.

Now, simply trust God to communicate to you. His

job is to speak so you can understand Him. God takes contracts and covenants very seriously. If you look back over the history of Israel, you will see that any time God entered into a contract with man, He was faithful to do His part. God's part is to be clear and understandable. You don't have to trust in your ability to hear God. Rather, you have to trust in His ability to communicate clearly. He is the one in the lead. He is the one taking responsibility to teach you to hear Him. And He is the one taking responsibility to speak to you. So He has the major part of the work.

Your job is to continue to be teachable. Press in to God in the areas of developing a close, intimate relationship with Him. Fulfill your commitment to obey Him once He does communicate something clearly to you.

When you asked God to teach you His voice, you asked Him for a good thing, didn't you? When you asked to hear His voice, did you think He would let you hear the enemy's voice instead? Will He give you a demon when you ask for the Holy Spirit? Of course not! He delights to give us good things when we ask for them.

In Luke 11:9–13, Jesus shows us that He desires to give good gifts to His people:

> So I say to you, ask, and it will be given to you; seek, and you will find; knock, and it will be opened to you. For everyone who asks receives, and he who seeks finds, and to him who knocks it will be opened. If a son asks for bread from any father among you, will he give him a stone? Or if he asks for a fish, will he give him a serpent instead of a fish? Or if he asks for an egg, will he offer him a scorpion? If you then, being evil, know how to give good gifts to your children,

how much more will your heavenly Father give the Holy Spirit to those who ask Him!

Jesus begins by inviting us to ask God for the things we need. Then He reminds us that natural parents do not give bad or hurtful things to their children when they ask for something. Finally He concludes with, "If you then, being evil, know how to give good gifts to your children, how much more will your heavenly Father give the Holy Spirit to those who ask Him." God is not going to allow a demon to control and mislead us when we are sincerely seeking to know His voice and to obey Him.

STEP 2—GIVE GOD A VOCABULARY TO SPEAK TO YOU.
This step is so basic that I almost missed it. Shortly after I had asked God to teach me His voice, I felt prompted to memorize Scripture. I spent about half an hour a day on it for months. As I read my Bible I wrote some of the verses on index cards, writing the reference on the reverse side of the card. Then I memorized the verses from the cards. I had no idea why I was doing it— I just felt strongly that God wanted me to do it, so I did.

When I first began to hear God's voice, often He called a scripture to my attention or brought a verse I'd memorized back to my memory.

One day I spent an hour struggling to memorize a difficult passage. I kept getting the phrases wrong or leaving parts out. I was growing frustrated. I decided just to give up and not bother memorizing any more verses. Then God spoke to me clearly—in my thoughts, not an audible voice. But it was so clear and sharp and distinct that I knew it was He. He said, "Teresa, you know the Bible is My Word. You want Me to speak directly to you. One of the main ways I speak to people is through My Word. When you memorize Scripture, you give Me a vocabulary to use when I speak to you."

I was astonished. I had not realized that by getting into His Word, studying it and memorizing portions of it, I was giving God a vocabulary to speak to me. As my hearing increased, God began to speak to me more on this subject. He said that when I spend time in His Word and spend time with Him, I get to know Him better. I get to know His nature and His behaviors, because He has revealed this about Himself in His Word. The more I know what God is like, the more I will understand what He would or would not say.

God also wanted me to increase my prayer and praise life. He wanted me to get to know His heart and to build a relationship with Him. That relationship, along with knowledge of Scripture, was giving God a vocabulary to speak to me.

Part of the key to hearing God's voice is giving Him the vocabulary in your life. A deep and thorough knowledge of Scripture is part of that vocabulary. Read it, meditate on it, study it, memorize it and ask God to talk to you about what a passage means. Also, look at God's character and nature as He has revealed Himself through His Word. Know what He is like, what He would or would not do, what He would or would not say.

Learning to put more depth into your relationship with God is another aspect of giving God a vocabulary to speak to you. Get to know Him experientially. Spend time with Him. You can do this in part by increasing your prayer and praise life. Ask God to show you His heart. Build your relationship together. Spend time each day just listening to what He has to say to you.

If we spend a lot of time around God, developing intimacy with Him and learning the Bible, then we will know His traits and characteristics. We will recognize His fragrance (so to speak). We will be able to discern His presence and will hear Him clearly when He speaks to us. The better we know Him, the easier it will be to recognize His voice. We will have given Him a vocabulary to speak to us.

STEP 3—GIVE YOURSELF PERMISSION TO MAKE MISTAKES.

As I stated earlier, learning God's voice is a process. Just like learning any new skill, you may be a bit clumsy at it at first, but you will improve with practice. Think back to a skill that you had to learn to do. Do you remember how awkward it felt at first? But now it is so easy.

I bet most of you are accomplished walkers. (There may be a few who read this book who have physical disabilities that keep them from walking.) But most of you can get up and walk across the room any time you want. Do you realize that was not always the case? There was a season when you had to learn to walk. You were not very good at it when you started. Look at a baby who is learning to walk. It stands up, takes a step, totters and falls on its rear end. What would happen if a baby stopped trying after the first fall or two? It would not learn to walk. But babies do not stop—they keep persisting. After a short season, they are running around the house. When babies become successful walkers, all the earlier frustrations of learning to walk are forgotten.

You no doubt have already gone through a process of learning to walk. You don't remember the early failures or mistakes you made as you learned to walk. It is like that in learning to hear God's voice. There will be some mistakes. There will be times when you "hear wrong." This is OK—it is part of the process. Give yourself permission to make mistakes and determine to keep going until you are successful.

I made some humorous mistakes when I first started trying to hear God. One Sunday I thought God told me to visit a certain church instead of going to my own church. I even heard the name of the church. So I looked it up in the phone book and wrote down the address. I looked up the address on a map and drove there. The street the church was on was only eight blocks long. I must have driven up and down that street forty times, and still I could not find the church. I spent nearly an hour looking for it.

I came home feeling frustrated and embarrassed. I knew I had heard wrong, and I felt like such an idiot. (Later I discovered that the street started and stopped several times. I had been driving on the wrong segment of the street.)

You may be OK with giving yourself permission to make some mistakes in the learning process. But you may have tried before to hear God's voice, and you believe that you failed miserably at your attempt. Maybe you've told yourself that you would never do that again. I have good news for you—you had been trying with the wrong equipment. It is now time to try again with the right equipment. This time it will be much easier.

I am reminded of when I learned to ice skate. When I first started, I had the wrong-sized boots, and they did not support my ankles. It was such a mess. When I got out on the ice, my ankles wobbled, and pretty soon things went sprawling. I knew I either had to grab the rail for support or fall down on the ice. It was embarrassing. I felt like such a klutz.

I left the ice and told myself that I would never try to skate again. But a more experienced skater came over

78

and talked to me about ice skate boots. I learned that they often run one to two sizes larger than regular shoe sizes. The skater suggested that if I wore a size eight shoe, I should try size six skates. I exchanged my rental skates for the right size, and the skater/advisor helped me tie them correctly. This time when I got back out on the ice, I may not have been an Olympic skater—but I could stand without my ankles wobbling. I could get around the rink with relatively few accidents. It was fun this time, and it motivated me to take lessons. My lessons began as raw beginner and progressed all the way through the advanced class.

Skating backward was not that difficult for me, but for a season I was convinced I would never master the art of stopping. I was hesitant to get up much speed because I did not know how to stop very well. Then I discovered ice dance. I worked on my basics (three-turns, mohawks, choctaws and others).

As I improved I hired a private coach. Later on I obtained a partner, and we eventually began entering amateur competitions in ice dance. I was still not Olympic caliber, but my skating was a vast improvement over where I started. I was now comfortable on the ice. I could start, stop, keep my balance, turn and go forward or backward with ease. By then it was so easy to skate that I hardly remembered the struggle it had been getting started.

You may have tried to hear God before, and failed miserably. You were just like me when I had on the wrong-sized skates. No matter how good and how sincere your efforts were, they were doomed to fail because you were using the wrong equipment. You may have "given up" just as I was about to do with ice skating, saying that you never want to try that again.

But look what happened for me. Someone came along and told me about the boot sizes and helped me get the right-sized boots. The right equipment made all the difference, and then I had a chance to really learn.

This book will help you to get the right-sized skates on. Now is the time to try again—you have the right equipment now. You will not be perfect when you first try, but you will find it is much easier and more doable now. So get back out there and do it! You will still have a learning curve, but you will be successful.

One final word of advice as you start: *Be persistent.* Jesus values persistence. He told several parables to emphasize that point. He talked about the persistent widow in Luke 18:1–5. He told us about the neighbor who kept bothering his friend in the middle of the night to borrow food for his unexpected guests in Luke 11:5–8. Jesus concluded that story by saying, "I say to you, though he will not rise and give to him because he is his friend, yet because of his persistence he will rise and give him as many as he needs" (v. 8).

The lesson from these stories is that God wants you to be persistent. Don't give up easily, and you will end up getting what you seek. You will learn to discern God's voice with a fair amount of accuracy.

Know in advance that you will make some mistakes. But do not give up. Just like the baby learning to walk for the first time, get back up and try again. Soon you will be "walking successfully all over the house" with your past mistakes totally forgotten. Remember, you entered into a contract with God. His part of the contract is to teach you. The Holy Spirit is an excellent teacher, and He is fully capable of doing His job. So you are in very good hands. God will see to it that you are successful in learning to hear His voice.

POINTS TO PONDER

1. What two things could you do to move into a closer and more intimate personal relationship with God?

2. Does the idea of committing to obey God appeal to you, or do you find it scary? Why is that?

3. What are some areas of your life where you think God will request lordship once you have committed to obey Him? Are you willing to turn them over to Him?

4. What are two or three practical steps you can do to position yourself to hear more clearly from God?

5. How do you feel about entering into a contract with God? Do you view this as a serious commitment? Do you believe God views this as a serious commitment? Do you believe He will keep His part of the contract?

6. How much time each day do you spend in fellowship with God? Realistically, how much time do you believe He wants you to spend in fellowship and intimacy with Him? Do the answers to these two questions line up fairly closely? If so, what can you do to keep it that way? If not, what realistic steps can you take to spend as much time with Him each day as He desires you to spend?

SEVEN

God's Style of Communication

In my early days of learning to hear God's voice, I had an experience that I hope you will never go through. Six or seven months after I started trying to hear God's voice, a friend told me about a church in Concord where the members were really good at hearing God's voice. Concord was an hour's drive from my home. But I was very hungry for God, and the pastor frequently taught on hearing God's voice, so I went to that church.

The pastor explained that God would first give you a picture or an image. Then you should press into God for an understanding of the image, which you could then share with others. It was amazing. Almost everyone at the church was getting images and pictures from God and hearing from Him.

I joined the church and was eager to hear God just as everyone else there did. But God never gave me any pictures. In fact, my hearing seemed to get worse, not better. At least God had spoken to me from time to time before I joined the church. Now He was not speaking to me at all. I became more and more frustrated.

The church did not own its own building. It rented a high school cafeteria and some nearby classrooms for Sunday school. About a year after I joined the church, I had a day of crisis. That morning, I attended a preservice prayer meeting in the kitchen. All the leaders from the church were there—the pastors, the home group leaders and the entire worship team. In addition there were a few "just-plain-old" intercessors like myself. Every single person in that prayer meeting was hearing God, with only one exception—me! They shared the pictures and words God was giving them. I dropped to my knees, squeezed my eyes closed and silently begged God to give me a picture.

Nothing!

Everyone in the room but me had received an image from the Lord and shared it with the group. I was so frustrated. The whole reason I was driving an hour each direction to church was to learn to hear God's voice. I had gone a whole year without hearing a single thing! I left the prayer meeting, went outside and wandered to the other end of the campus. I went behind the gymnasium and cried out to God in anguish, "GOD! God, where are You? Why aren't You speaking to me?"

To my surprise He answered me, clearly and distinctly in my thoughts. He said, "Teresa, I have been trying to speak to you for the whole last year, but you have not been listening to Me!"

I was stunned. "But God," I said, "how can that be? I have not received a single picture."

He replied, "That is because I was not using pictures to speak to you."

Then I realized what had happened. I was so intent

that God had to speak to me in a certain way that I ignored any other way that God might speak to me. I had spent a whole year in needless frustration because I was looking for pictures while God was patiently speaking to me in a still, small voice in my "mind's ear." I unconsciously blocked that out and assumed it was not God because it was not the picture that I was looking for. I was listening for God to speak to me only one way, but He had chosen to speak to me a different way. All the time I thought He was being silent, He had been speaking to me. I was the one who was not listening and therefore not hearing Him.

THE SOUND OF GOD'S VOICE

What does God's voice sound like? Many people answer that by saying it is the still, small voice that Elijah heard in 1 Kings 19:11–13. Let's look at that passage:

> Then He [God] said, "Go out and stand on the mountain before the LORD." And behold, the LORD passed by, and a great and strong wind tore into the mountains and broke the rocks in pieces before the LORD, but the LORD was not in the wind; and after the wind an earthquake, but the LORD was not in the earthquake; and after the earthquake a fire, but the LORD was not in the fire; and after the fire a still small voice.
>
> So it was, when Elijah heard it, that he wrapped his face in his mantle and went out and stood in the entrance of the cave. Suddenly a voice came to him and said, "What are you doing here, Elijah?"

From this passage, we learn that God was not in the wind. God was not in the fire, and He was not in the earthquake. The passage tells us that when God speaks to us, He uses a still, small voice. So, if we want to hear Him, we should listen for that still, small voice, right? Actually...wrong. (I set you up on that one. Sorry.) There is another passage of scripture from a bit before Elijah's time. It happened just as the Lord led His people out of Egyptian bondage, parted the Red Sea for them to cross safely and then destroyed the army that was pursuing them by closing the Red Sea on the enemy. After that, God told Moses that He wanted to enter into covenant with the people of Israel. He wanted to be their God, and He wanted them to be His people.

Moses took this offer to the leaders of the tribes. The leaders of the tribes took it to those in their tribes. The answer came back—*yes!* Yes, they wanted to be God's people, to be set apart for Him and to serve Him as their God.

So God arranged to meet with them. The people spent two days preparing for this meeting, both physically and spiritually. Then the day arrived and...well, let's pick up the story directly from Scripture:

> On the morning of the third day there was thunder and lightning, with a thick cloud over the mountain, and a very loud trumpet blast. Everyone in the camp trembled. Then Moses led the people out of the camp to meet with God, and they stood at the foot of the mountain. Mount Sinai was covered with smoke, because the Lord descended on it in fire. The smoke billowed up from it like smoke from a furnace, the whole mountain trembled violently, and the sound of the trumpet grew louder and louder. Then Moses spoke and the voice of God answered him.
>
> —EXODUS 19:16–19, NIV

85

Wait a minute! We just learned in 1 Kings 19 that God was not in the fire, and He was not in the earthquake. But here we see God was in the fire, and He was in the earthquake. In 1 Kings 19, God spoke in a still, small voice. But here in Exodus 19, He spoke in a huge, booming voice, loud enough for the masses of people gathered around the base of the mountain to hear Him! The Bible says that the people He brought out of Egypt were a multitude, very large in number. If each of them could all hear God at the same time, that must have been one very loud voice!

We have just seen God use two vastly different styles of communication—one for Elijah, and another for Moses and the people of Israel. God is a very creative God, and He finds many different ways to speak to His children. If Elijah had put God in a box and listened only for the booming voice that God used on Mount Sinai, he would have missed God's gentle whisper.

God will use different ways to speak to us. He spoke quietly in a conversational method to me that day in Concord, silently in my thoughts. But He showed the pastor of the church pictures in his mind's eye. At that time, I did not get pictures at all. Since then, God has sometimes used pictures with me. Sometimes He speaks to me in that still, small voice. Sometimes He drops something in my spirit, and I "just know." God uses many different communication styles, and He will often use more than just one style with each of us.

GOD HAS A PRIMARY WAY OF SPEAKING TO EACH PERSON

God has a primary way of speaking to each of us for

86

the "big stuff." In other words, He may have several different ways that He communicates to you, but when the "stakes are high," He has a primary way of communicating to use with you so that you can recognize it is He. He used pictures for that pastor. With me, the Holy Spirit drops something directly into my spirit, and I "just know" with confidence, details and accuracy.

Using two incidents from Peter's life, let's look at God's primary communication style with him. In the first incident, Jesus communicated His lordship to Peter (Luke 5:4–8). Let's set the time frame and understand the context. Jesus wanted to do some teaching. Multitudes had followed Him. He was on the shore of a lake, where the shore sloped upward to a mountainside. Jesus understood that the best way to address the crowd so that everyone could hear Him was to go a bit out onto the water. If the people sat on the slopes, it would form a natural amphitheater.

Peter was a fisherman and had a boat, so Jesus asked Peter to take Him out from shore a bit so He could address the crowd. After He finished teaching, He "paid" Peter for the use of his boat. Let's pick up the story from Scripture:

> When he had finished speaking, he said to Simon, "Put out into deep water, and let down the nets for a catch."
>
> Simon answered, "Master, we've worked hard all night and haven't caught anything. But because you say so, I will let down the nets."
>
> When they had done so, they caught such a large number of fish that their nets began to break. So they signaled their partners in the other boat to come and help them, and they came and

filled both boats so full that they began to sink.
When Simon Peter saw this, he fell at Jesus'
knees and said, "Go away from me, Lord; I am a
sinful man!"

—LUKE 5:4–8, NIV

Now, Peter's reaction would seem out of place if we
do not realize precisely what Jesus is communicating
to him. By backing up a bit in Peter's life we can
understand the full impact of Jesus' actions.

In John 1:29–42, Peter first meets Jesus on the day
after John the Baptist baptized Jesus. Jesus was baptized, then verse 35 says that "the next day" Andrew
began to follow Jesus. The first thing Andrew did was
to go get his brother Simon (Peter) and bring him to
Jesus. Verse 42 tells us that Jesus accepted Peter as one
of His followers.

These chronological events took place before Jesus
sat in Peter's boat to teach the crowds (Luke 5:3).
Peter already knew Jesus. But at that point he did not
fully understand who Jesus was. He was willing to follow Jesus in his spare time, but he had not yet given up
his profession of fishing (v. 2).

The nets filled with fish is an interesting miracle. In it,
Jesus met Peter at Peter's level. Peter was a professional
fisherman and considered himself skilled and knowledgeable. Yet, with all his experience as a fisherman,
Peter was unable to catch any fish that day. That means
they simply were not "catchable!" Yet Jesus caused Peter
to catch a greater measure of fish than he had ever seen
caught before in his life! Peter had just been made successful beyond his own natural abilities. And his success
came as a result of accessing the power of God by
responding to God's direction about something Peter

already know how to do. This miracle gave Peter a revelation of who Jesus really was—God incarnate, the Lord of all creation. Peter became aware of Jesus' holiness and of the stark contrast of his own sinful and fallen nature. This is why he said, "Go away from me, Lord; I am a sinful man!" (v. 8, NIV).

But Jesus did not depart from him. Jesus' response is very important. He told Peter, "Don't be afraid; from now on you will catch men" (v. 10, NIV). Immediately after Peter's revelation of who Jesus really was, Jesus commissioned him into full-time ministry. This was very significant to Peter, as indicated by his response. He pulled his boat (his livelihood) to the shore, left everything and wholeheartedly followed Jesus (v. 11).

This miracle of the "impossible fish catch" was the primary method by which Jesus spoke to Peter. The method involved empowering Peter supernaturally in an area where he already had considerable natural ability. By this Peter received an understanding of who Jesus was, received a commission into ministry and found that his whole life had been changed.

Things went well for Peter for about three years. As part of the inner circle of disciples, he was able to see Jesus transformed on the mountaintop. He was sent out with power and authority to heal the sick and cast out demons. Peter felt pretty good about his ministry calling. Then one day the unthinkable happened. Jesus was arrested.

Just a short time before Jesus' arrest, Peter had sworn allegiance to Jesus, saying, "I will lay down my life for Your sake" (John 13:37). But when he was identified as one of the disciples, Peter denied—three times—that he even knew Jesus (Luke 22:54–60). As soon he did this, the cock crowed, just as Jesus predicted. Then Jesus turned His head and looked directly at Peter (v. 61). Peter realized that Jesus knew what he had done. If ever he had a reason to feel disqualified from ministry, this was it! He ran out of the courtyard, weeping bitterly (v. 62).

From Peter's perspective, his bad behavior had just caused him to be forever disqualified from ministry. He felt he had placed a giant "null and void" over God's call on his life. It was all over for Peter—his hopes, dreams and ambitions in God destroyed in a single instant.

We see that from that point on, Peter gave up on God's call on his life. He returned to his old profession of fishing (John 21:3), even though Jesus had risen from the dead and appeared to Peter (20:19). My guess is that Peter was afraid to make eye contact with God, still remembering how Jesus had looked squarely at him when he denied Him. My guess is that he was so overcome with guilt and shame that he was not able to understand what it really meant for Jesus to rise from the dead.

Peter was at a point of crisis. He had given up everything to follow Jesus. But now he felt totally disqualified from ministry. He believed that God was mad at him. Things looked hopeless from Peter's perspective. If ever he needed to hear clearly from God, it was then.

So God decided to speak to him using the primary method of communication He usually used with Peter. He spoke to Peter in the same manner as when He first revealed His lordship to Peter. Let's look at this in John 21:3–8:

> "I'm going out to fish," Simon Peter told them, and they said, "We'll go with you." So they went out and got into the boat, but that night they caught nothing.
>
> Early in the morning, Jesus stood on the shore,

but the disciples did not realize that it was Jesus. He called out to them, "Friends, haven't you any fish?"

"No," they answered.

He said, "Throw your net on the right side of the boat and you will find some." When they did, they were unable to haul the net in because of the large number of fish.

Then the disciple whom Jesus loved said to Peter, "It is the Lord!" As soon as Simon Peter heard him say, "It is the Lord," he wrapped his outer garment around him (for he had taken it off) and jumped into the water. The other disciples followed in the boat, towing the net full of fish, for they were not far from shore, about a hundred yards.

—NIV

Do you understand the dynamic here? Peter thought he was disqualified and rejected by God. Yet Jesus met him in the same way that He met Peter when He first revealed His lordship to Peter. That earlier meeting had been followed by a commissioning. Now He once again revealed His lordship to Peter, and Peter was so drawn to Jesus that he could not wait for the boat to get back to shore. He jumped in the water and swam to Jesus. There on the shore, face to face with Jesus, Jesus restored Peter's ministry commission. "Feed My lambs," Jesus told Peter (John 21:15). In other words, Jesus was telling Peter to care for the babes in the faith. Peter was being restored to his pastoral role.

Jesus also told Peter, "Tend My sheep" (v. 16). Jesus was telling Peter to gather in the sheep—that is doing the work of an evangelist. Along with that would come signs and wonders, such as the biblical record of

Peter's shadow imparting healing to the sick!

Finally Jesus told Peter, "Feed My sheep" (v. 17). Here He told Peter he would be involved in teaching and the establishing of doctrine. Through these communications from Jesus to Peter, Peter was fully restored to the very ministry he had given up.

When the stakes were high and Peter desperately needed to hear clearly from God, God used His primary communication style with Peter. This is what Peter recognized and how Peter could know it was really God.

God will develop a primary communication style with each of us. But He may speak to us in many other ways as well. The primary way He communicates with me may not be the way He communicates with you. But when God wants you to know for sure that it is He speaking to you, He will probably use the primary communication method that He established with you earlier. Knowing the primary method He uses with you will make it easier to recognize His voice when you really need to hear Him.

That is the reason it is so important to learn to hear God in the little stuff. Then you will learn how God communicates with you. And you will be able to recognize Him clearly in the big stuff—those times when you really need to hear Him.

SPECIALIZING HIS COMMUNICATION WITH US

In today's technological world, communication methods are becoming more and more specialized every day. God also specializes His communication. He will use different methods of communication with you, depending on the topic that He wants to talk to you about. In some things, God will speak loudly and clearly—and there will be no doubt as to what He is communicating to you. But in other communications, you may experience a different degree of accuracy in hearing and discerning what God is saying. Let me share from my own experiences.

God communicates to me in three different ways. I have varying levels of confidence in the accuracy of my hearing, depending on which style He is using.

Sometimes God speaks to me "deep to deep." He will drop something in my spirit, and I will know it with absolute confidence. The clarity of the communication seems to resonate within my very being. When God speaks to me in this manner, I am willing to bet my life on what I have heard and to obey instantly. So far I have had 100 percent accuracy in hearing correctly and clearly when He speaks this way.

When I am in a ministry setting, and hearing God "for others," God will frequently speak to me by what I call "just knowing." It is as if He has suddenly dropped an encyclopedia in me, and I know all sorts of facts about the person. When I test these facts (by sharing what I know with the person), they turn out to be accurate, but I have no idea how I know those details. I would say that my accuracy in this style of hearing is somewhere between 90 to 95 percent. Occasionally I make mistakes or "miss it," but that is pretty rare. I have a pretty high degree of confidence in hearing God when He speaks to me this way. But I do make allowances for the fact that I could occasionally hear wrong.

Finally, when God speaks to me for personal fellowship, I usually "hear" Him conversationally. This sounds very much like my own thoughts, and I find myself asking the question more frequently, "Lord, was that really You, or was it just me?" I would say my hearing on the personal fellowship level is only about 85 percent accurate. When I first started hearing Him this way, I was only about 50 percent accurate. I am still working with the Lord on this, hoping to reach a higher level of accuracy.

The Lord constantly speaks to me in this way. I find He is a very conversational God. He loves to initiate and hold conversations with me.

Sometimes God explains things to me in our time alone together. Sometimes He talks to me about changes He wants to make in my character and nature to help me grow. He has spoken to me about mistakes I've made and what He wants me to do to correct them. Sometimes He talks to me about my ministry or about my job. Sometimes He reveals things to me about Himself. Sometimes He plays jokes on me. Sometimes He tells me minor things that are going to happen—shortly before they do happen. One time while attending a football game, He kept telling me how many yards my team was going to make on their next down. And He was right each time. (I tried to get Him to tell me hints about which stocks would perform well on the stock market, but He just laughed at me!) When God and I fellowship, He usually speaks to me conversationally in that still, small voice.

The point of my sharing this with you is so you will recognize some of the communication styles God may use with you. You will begin to notice that you have varying levels of accuracy in your hearing, depending on which style God is using. You will also recognize the one primary style He uses to communicate with you, and you will have a high degree of confidence in your hearing through that style. You will also discover the style He uses when communicating with you on the really *big stuff*.

94

POINTS TO PONDER

1. Have you ever had a time when you desperately wanted God to speak to you but He did not seem to do so? Thinking back on that time, were you expecting God to speak to you in a certain way? Is it possible that He was answering you in another way, but you did not recognize it because you were looking for Him to speak in one specific way?

2. Have you noticed God speaking to you in more than one style? Do you have more confidence in your hearing of God in certain areas or styles than you do in others?

3. Have you noticed a primary communication style that God uses with you for the really big stuff?

4. How does God communicate with you during your day-to-day fellowship and devotions with Him? Does He use that same way when you are seeking His response for a topic you consider critical, or does He use another manner of communication then?

EIGHT

"God, Is That Really You?"

H ave you ever thought God was saying something to you, but you were not sure it was really His voice you were hearing? Have you found yourself thinking, *How do I know it was really God I heard and not my own imagination or the enemy?*

When we ask that question, we are really asking for wisdom and discernment. We need God's wisdom to discern if it was really God's voice we just heard. Fortunately, God has already provided a solution in His Word to this dilemma. James 1:5 says, "If any of you lacks wisdom, let him ask of God, who gives to all liberally and without reproach, and it will be given to him."

God's solution is so simple we almost miss it: If we need to know if we are hearing His voice, all we have to do is ask Him! He will tell us. Tell Him what you think you just heard Him say, and then ask Him to please confirm it or correct your hearing on the matter.

God eagerly looks for people who desire to know and

understand His voice. He is eager to meet them and teach them.

> The Lord looks down from heaven upon the children of men, to see if there are any who understand, who seek God.
>
> —PSALM 14:2

In Psalm 119:26–29, David shares his secret for hearing God's voice. David went back to God for understanding on what he heard God say, and then he prayerfully pondered it. In verses 26–27, David states:

> I have declared my ways, and You answered me; teach me Your statutes. Make me understand the way of Your precepts; so shall I meditate on Your wonderful works.

These verses show clearly that God will teach us His statutes (His ways and His voice) if we set ourselves apart to seek Him. In short, when we ask God, He gives us the clarity we need. There are more scriptural precedents about asking God for wisdom to discern His voice that can be found in Proverbs 2:2–7 and Psalm 119:73, 124–125.

God wants to give us an understanding of what He is saying to us, because He wants to communicate with us. He knows it can be frightening for us as we begin venturing out in hearing and obeying Him. He knows we need confirmation from Him, and He is more than willing to have us discuss with Him what we believe He said to us.

FLEECING GOD

There is an important thing to know about the process of confirming God's voice. We must not give God an ultimatum about how He is to confirm His word to us. That is called "putting a fleece before the Lord." The concept of fleecing God comes from an experience Gideon had when he was trying to sort out the call of God on His life. (See Judges 6:11–14.)

Gideon had an angelic visitation, during which he was told that God had chosen him to save all Israel from the Midianites. Gideon was instructed to tear down the altar of Baal, but he was timid, so he did it secretly by night. He was not feeling very confident in his calling—or in his hearing from God. Then the Midianites gathered against Israel with a huge army. Gideon was desperate to know for sure that God was with him and would deliver Israel by His hand just as He had told Gideon He would do.

Gideon went back to God to double-check his hearing. (See Judges 6:36–40.) First he laid a fleece (sheepskin) on the threshing floor and asked God to make the dew come only on the fleece—and not on the ground around the fleece. God did this for him. But poor Gideon got overinvolved in analyzing God's response. He reasoned that it would have been better to do the test in the opposite way. So the next night he asked God to reconfirm His word to him by covering the ground with dew, but leaving the fleece dry. Once again, God did as Gideon requested; He wanted Gideon to be confident in his calling and able to perform the tasks God had given Him to do.

When reading that passage, some people assume they can tell God precisely how to confirm or correct what they believe they have heard Him say to them. In essence, they believe they are allowed to dictate the "supernatural hoops" through which God must jump to prove He really said what they believe they heard.

God allowed Gideon to fleece Him, but there is a strong scriptural precedent against telling God specifically what to do. In Job 40:2, Job is rebuked for commanding God. In Psalm 78:17–18, the Lord calls it outright rebellion when the Israelites "willfully put God to the test by demanding the food they craved" (NIV). Psalm 78:41 says that God finds it vexing when we test Him. And Jesus Himself refused Satan's suggestion to put a fleece or test before God by casting Himself off of the highest point of the temple. In both Matthew 4:7 and Luke 4:12, Jesus said, "Do not put the Lord your God to the test" (NIV).

When we go back to God for confirmation, we need to allow Him to choose how He corrects or confirms what we heard. It is not our place to dictate how He does this. Instead we must trust that He will do it in a way we can clearly recognize as Him.

PUT YOUR FAITH IN THE RIGHT THING

When I was first learning to hear God's voice, I went overboard in my need to double-check my hearing with God. I struggled with knowing whether God would lovingly and gently correct me if I heard wrong and wandered astray in my attempt to obey Him. I was so afraid that I might hear wrong and go "off the deep end." I worried that I might do the wrong thing when I thought I was obeying God, then I would *get in trouble* with God. I didn't want Him to have to punish or rebuke me for my mistake.

As a result, I tended to check and recheck my hearing on just about everything. I became very sluggish in obeying God, because I spent so much time verifying everything that I heard. It was crippling my ability to be effective in my calling.

My basic problem was that I had placed my faith in the wrong thing. I was looking to and trusting in *my ability to hear God* instead of in *His ability (and faithfulness) to speak clearly* and to redirect me if I heard wrong. It took me a while to learn that God really is faithful to correct, and that His corrections are not something to be afraid of.

I used to think that "correction" was the same as "punishment." But God revamped my thinking on that by reminding me of my ice skating coach. I really liked him, and he was very helpful. He never made me feel stupid or put me down. Instead he helped me to improve my skating. He would watch me try to execute a move, and then offer feedback, saying something like, "Your weight is drifting to the left when you turn. You need to keep it balanced over your skating foot." I had just been corrected, but not put down or made to feel small or punished. The intent of the correction was to help me excel. I became a fairly good skater because my coach was faithful to tell me if I did something wrong and how to fix it. I applied what he told me, and as a result, my skating improved.

God told me to look to Him as my coach. He promised that He would let me know when I got something wrong and how to correct it so I could excel in Him. Suddenly correction became something to be desired instead of something to be feared.

Don't fear the Lord's correction in the process of learning to recognize His voice. His motivation is not to punish your mistakes but to help you excel. If you have heard correctly and go back to Him for confirmation, He will reassure you that you did indeed hear Him. If you heard incorrectly, He will give you clarity on what He is really saying on the subject. His desire is for you to excel in hearing Him clearly and accurately. He loves you, and He wants to communicate with you very much.

You will grow in confidence as He corrects you when you hear wrong. As you experience His gentle and loving correction, you will begin to realize just how faithful He is and how much He is committed to the process of teaching you His voice. After a while, you will not have to go back and recheck your hearing as often.

HEARING HIM IN DIFFICULT AREAS

We need to remember that there are certain areas were our hearing is likely to be less accurate and where it is harder to hear God's voice clearly. It is more difficult to hear God clearly when we have "big stakes" in the subject, where our hearts are tremendously engaged or in areas where we already know we have a history of hearing wrong. We must double-check these areas and ask God to confirm what we heard.

Let me share an example from a friend who hears pretty well in most areas of her life. She recently went through a divorce. After a few months of a "recovery period," she began to get involved in various Christian activities, although she was still very lonely. She met a single man who seemed to be everything she wanted in a husband. She thought she began to hear God speak to her about this man, telling her that indeed he was the man God had for her.

She was excited about it and told me what she had heard. I suspected strongly that this was her own heart, and I tried to find a gentle way to tell her this. But she thought God was saying more and more detailed things to her. She thought she heard Him tell her that this man would ask her to marry him in December. She heard that her Christmas present would be an engagement ring, with the wedding following shortly after that. She was so sure it was God's voice.

But in reality it was her own heart telling her what she longed to hear. December came and went, and she did not receive any Christmas present from this man— much less an engagement ring. She was sorely disappointed and a bit confused. So she asked God for guidance, and she felt God wanted her to talk to the man. She decided that this man was too shy to follow through on God's promptings to ask her to marry him. She believed he needed some encouragement.

So she sat down with him and shared her deep feelings for him. She was surprised and hurt to learn that he did not have similar feelings for her—he considered her a casual friend, and that was it.

My friend was devastated that the man was not interested in her. But she was even more dismayed about how wrong she had been in hearing God's voice. She thought she was pretty good at hearing the Lord, and in general, she does hear very well. She did not understand how she could mishear so totally in this particular area. It shook her confidence in hearing God in any area for a season.

She did not realize that we are more likely to mishear God in an area where our hearts are highly engaged, where we are emotionally involved. She did not recognize her own heart imitating God's voice to her. She did not double-check her hearing with God, because she so desperately wanted to hear what she heard.

In a similar vein, I suspect my hearing regarding the friend I mentioned in a previous chapter. I trust my hearing in a lot of areas, but when God says something to me about this friend, I know I have to go back and recheck my hearing. As a matter of fact, my heart is so engaged on the subject of this friendship that I often ask someone whose hearing I trust to help me sort out what I hear regarding the friendship. I know I am very weak in hearing God in that one particular area, so I usually look to others whom I trust for help.

SCRIPTURAL PRECEDENTS

It is wise to get into the habit of checking what God says to you against Scripture. God will not say something to us that is contradictory to what the Bible says. There will be certain things we can eliminate immediately as "not from God" when we line them up against what God has already said in the Bible.

But there are many areas that the Bible does not seem to address explicitly. Did you know that many times God is willing to give us a scriptural precedent for what He said to us? For instance, let's look at a hypothetical case. Imagine you are trying to decide which of two job offers God wants you to accept. You believe He tells you to take job offer two, one which will put you in contact with hurting people to whom you can minister.

But job offer two is a much lower-paying job than job offer one, so you want to be sure you are hearing God. You ask Him for a confirmation, a scriptural precedent. As you try to make a decision, God directs your attention to the words of Jesus in the Gospels: "Those who are well have no need of a physician, but those who are sick. I did not come to call the righteous, but sinners, to repentance." (See Matthew 9:12–13; Mark 2:17; Luke 5:31.)

103

God has just given you a scriptural principle that He sent Jesus to those who needed His help and were willing to receive it. This scriptural precedent lets you know you have received the confirmation that you have heard Him speak to you to take job offer two.

God likes to use scriptural precedence as one of the ways by which He confirms His communication to us.

THE AREA OF ASSUMPTION

There is another area where we need to be very careful when hearing God's voice. This is the area of assumption. God can speak to us very clearly, and we can hear Him accurately. But there can be times when we make an assumption about *what He means* and discover later that *we were not correct.* We have to be very careful not to put words in God's mouth or make assumptions about what He says.

Let me give you an example that I heard in a teaching tape by Dr. Bill Hamon of Christian International. There was a season of Dr. Hamon's ministry when he purchased some property and began a building project. At first there was plenty of funding for it, but after a while, the funds ran out. He began earnestly praying for the Lord to supply the money.

God told him clearly, "Son, I will not allow that which is most precious to you to be lost." Bill assumed that God was talking about the building project since that was very precious to him and was the subject about which he had been praying for God's direction. But the funds never came in, and the bank repossessed the property.

About the same time, Bill's daughter went through a serious health crisis, and he had to nurse her back to health. It seemed he faced one crisis on top of another.

Bill was devastated that the property had been lost, particularly because he believed God had explicitly told him that He would not allow that which was most precious to Bill to be lost. After a period of time, God finally explained to him, "Son, when I was talking about that which was most precious to you, I was not talking about the property. I was talking about your daughter."

Let me share one last example in the area of assumption. Recently a close friend of mine received a prophetic word from a lady she met on the Internet, one who seemed to be very gifted. Kari* had been seeking the Lord to talk to her about a crisis she was facing. Her older sister, who was also a spiritual mentor to her, had become angry with her and had stopped speaking to my friend. She would not return phone calls, e-mails or letters or engage in any form of communication. Kari was heartbroken and spent weeks praying about the problem with her sister. She sought direction from God.

This online prophet told Kari that she had received a picture of Kari on her knees, praying and crying, wrapped in a soft blue blanket. A thread had come loose in the picture, and the blanket unraveled until it was completely gone. Kari had been holding onto the thread, but when she released it to God's hands, something happened. Suddenly Kari was again wrapped in the blanket, and it was fully restored.

The prophet understood that the blanket represented an important relationship that had been falling apart. The prophet said that God would restore that relationship after Kari "let go" and turned it over to God. It was an accurate and keen word.

But assumption crept in at this point: The prophet assumed that the important relationship was the

---

* Not her real name.

relationship between Kari and her husband instead of between Kari and her sister. She began to minister to Kari about it.

Now, Kari's relationship with her husband was very solid. As soon as the prophet shared the picture of the blue blanket, Kari believed the blanket unraveling represented her relationship with her sister—not with her husband. So she asked the prophet if it were possible that it was about her sister, not her husband. To the prophet's credit, she agreed that the blanket could indeed be the sister. She gave Kari some very quality ministry regarding the situation with her sister.

The prophet had received a very keen word from God about Kari's situation in the form of a picture. But the power of that word was almost diluted when she assumed the relationship was a spouse. This is an example of how we can accurately hear from God and then make assumptions that mislead us—and those to whom we speak. We want to be careful to avoid doing that!

THE ROLE OF OBEDIENCE

While we are on the subject of determining whether or not it is really God's voice, let's look at how obedience falls into the equation. Let me introduce the concept of *cheap* vs. *expensive* obedience.

Cheap obedience is obeying when the stakes are not very high, when it does not cost much to obey. For instance, remember my opening story in chapter one? I thought I'd have a twenty-minute wait after I missed my bus. But God told me not to sit down and to look at my watch because another bus was coming in less than five minutes. It really did not matter whether or not that was really God's voice; there was no risk in obeying that command. I could safely remain standing for five minutes. I could watch the time, because there were not any big stakes in doing that. That is an example of cheap, or low-risk, obedience.

Expensive obedience involves some real consequences to obeying God. The story in chapter six where God asked me to give a pastor the money to buy an engagement ring for his fiancée is an example of expensive obedience. If God were not really telling me to do that, there would be big consequences to me because it was a large sum of money (several thousand dollars).

Be sure you have heard from God before you do something that could ask you to give expensive obedience. Expensive obedience is not limited to money—it can be involved any time the stakes are high. If you believe God is telling you to terminate a relationship because it is unhealthy, that is *expensive obedience* because a relationship that is important to you is at risk if you have heard wrong.

If the obedience is low cost or low risk, then you should always and instantly obey. It may very well be God speaking to you, and you want to be in the habit of obeying God instantly. On the other hand, if it involves expensive obedience, then you need to double-check your hearing and be sure it is God speaking to you before you obey.

This is an important guideline to follow: The more costly the stakes of obedience, the more important it is to make sure you have heard God clearly before obeying. On the other hand, the more trivial the stakes, the more you want to be in the habit of practicing instant obedience rather than spending a great deal of time double-checking with God before you obey Him.

POINTS TO PONDER

1. Have you ever had an experience where you thought God spoke something to you, but you were not sure whether or not it was really He? What did you do to sort it out? Did you finally act upon it, or did you simply let it pass?

2. Do you think more people find it hard to be sure it is really God's voice they hear? Or do you think more people are pretty sure it is God's voice they hear when He speaks to them?

3. Have you ever had a time when your own heart imitated God's voice to you? How did you finally figure out that it was not really God's voice?

4. Have you ever double-checked with God on your hearing and received confirmation? If so, how did God confirm His voice to you?

5. Is it a good thing or a bad thing when God corrects us? Why?

6. Has there been a time in your life when God corrected you? What was it like? How did He do this? How did you feel about the experience?

7. Can you give an example from your own life of a situation that God brought to you that required low-cost obedience? Can you give an example from your own experiences of a situation requiring expensive or high-cost obedience?

NINE

What God's Voice Does Not Sound Like

An important step in learning to recognize God's voice is understanding what His voice *does not sound like*. There are certain things we can eliminate immediately because we know God's voice does not sound that way. We will look at some of the ways God's voice will not sound like in this chapter.

GOD WILL NOT SAY ANYTHING THAT CONTRADICTS SCRIPTURE

In chapter 3 we thoroughly discussed the fact that God will not contradict Scripture. Let's review those facts. God has spoken to us through the Bible; it is His Word. He does not contradict Himself, so He would not say something that contradicts what He has already said in the Bible.

If you ever think you have *heard* God tell you something that contradicts Scripture, then you can be assured that you have heard wrong. He won't do that. Go back to God, tell Him what you thought you heard and ask Him to show you what He really has to say about that issue.

GOD'S VOICE IS NOT THE VOICE OF ANXIETY, UNSETTLEDNESS OR EXHAUSTION

God is the God of peace. In John 14:27, Jesus said, "Peace I leave with you, My peace I give to you; not as the world gives do I give to you. Let not your heart be troubled, neither let it be afraid."

Our thinking and our walk with God is to be earmarked by His peace: "For to be carnally minded is death, but to be spiritually minded is life and peace" (Rom. 8:6). The Bible clearly states that confusion (or unsettledness) is not of God: "For God is not the author of confusion but of peace, as in all the churches of the saints" (1 Cor. 14:33).

The word *peace* is mentioned over a hundred times in the New Testament, so it must be pretty important to God. The word *rest* (used in the context of relaxing, being refreshed and not exhausted) is used twenty-nine times in the New Testament. In fact, when Jesus saw that His disciples were worn out and exhausted from too demanding a ministry schedule, He said to them, "Come aside by yourselves to a deserted place and rest a while" (Mark 6:31). The verse continues by saying, "For there were many coming and going, and they did not even have time to eat."

God's presence—and His voice—are earmarked by peace and rest. When you become exhausted or anxious, it is more difficult to hear Him clearly. No doubt you have experienced this in your day-to-day life. Think of a time when you were very tired. All you wanted to do was sleep, but you had a friend who was trying to talk to you. You probably had a hard time concentrating on what that person was saying because you were so exhausted! When you are very tired it is much harder to follow a conversation than when you are rested.

The same principle applies when we listen to God. God desires for us to walk in His rest and peace. When we are anxious or unsettled, or when we are exhausted, it is harder to hear His voice.

For a long time I would cry out for God to speak to me late at night after a long hard day. Almost every time this happened, God did not answer me until the next morning. I began to think God always made me wait overnight for an answer. I assumed it had something to do with the concept of waiting on the Lord.

Later I discovered that was not the case at all. One day I asked God, "Why do You always delay Your answer until the next day?"

God sat me down and explained it to me. He told me that most of the time when I came to Him late at night, I was exhausted and therefore unable to hear Him clearly. At those times He put me to sleep, gave me rest and put me in a place where I was able to hear Him more clearly. Then, when I was in a listening place, He talked to me about the things for which I was seeking Him.

It is the same when we are anxious. When our minds are racing with anxiety, it is harder to hear God clearly.

One of the early church fathers once said something to the effect of, "Get your direction from God when you are in a place where you can hear Him clearly. Do not change direction when you are in a state of turmoil. Keep operating on the last clear directions you had until you are back to a place where you can hear God clearly for new directions." There is great wisdom in that.

God does not speak to us from a place of anxiety and unsettledness. Instead, He helps us deal with the things that got us in that state and gives us His peace. Then He will speak to us clearly. He does not speak to us from a place of exhaustion. Instead, He has us rest and get our balance back, and then He speaks clearly to us.

GOD'S VOICE IS NOT THE VOICE OF OBSCURITY

People sometimes make it a lot harder to hear God than it should be. They think God is going to talk to them in obscure riddles or by other cryptic means. They assume that He will be hard to understand. That is not what the Bible says. James 1:5 tells us that God gives those who seek Him wisdom to hear His voice clearly.

Have you ever seen the Indiana Jones movie where Jones is searching for the Holy Grail? In that movie, the main characters found a series of clues in an ancient language, which they translated. It turned out to be a series of obscure riddles—only someone clever and diligent would be able to figure it out. The average man would not have a prayer of a chance. To make matters worse, there were some very high price tags attached to the riddles—if you did not guess right or weren't quick enough, you would pay with your life.

One of the riddles said, "Only the penitent shall pass." Indiana Jones walked along a passageway, muttering to himself, "Only the penitent shall pass. Only the penitent shall pass. Only the penitent shall pass." Suddenly he realized that penitent men approach God *on their knees*, so he dropped to his knees. The very next instant a giant axe came swinging out from a wall and would have chopped him in half if he had still been standing. But since he had dropped to his knees, the axe passed over his head. He had figured out that riddle in just the nick of time! If he had taken a second longer to figure it out, it would have cost him his life.

Some of us view God's voice in a way very similar to this Indiana Jones movie depiction. We think that God is very obscure. We believe it is a difficult task to figure out what God desires to communicate. We think it is far beyond the average Christian's ability to do so. That simply is not true.

There is a test that comes with hearing God, but it is not about our *ability to discern* what He is saying. He is willing to communicate clearly to us. The test is in our *willingness to obey* God once we have heard Him clearly. In John 14:15, Jesus says, "If you love me, you will obey what I command" (NIV). God will communicate clearly to us if we will listen to what He tells us and obey Him. His ability to communicate is greater than our ability to "miss it" or "hear wrong."

GOD'S VOICE IS NOT
THE VOICE OF GOSSIP

I originally learned this concept from a teaching by John Webster, one that I would like to share with you:

> God hates gossip. I would like to define gossip for you. Gossip is not simply a bad report or a falsehood. Gossip is when you talk about anything when you are not part of the problem or the solution. It can be true, correct, right as far as the factual report, but if it doesn't concern you and you are talking about it anyway, it is gossip. God did not intend for us to talk about the issues of our

113

neighbor's life unless we are part of the problem or solution. Otherwise, we should stay out of it. You can be real glad that God is not a gossip. That gives you the safety of knowing that God is not going to talk to your friend or neighbor about your personal problems unless they are part of the problem or solution. God is not a talebearer. He just does not go around talking to others about the problems that you are having in your life.[1]

God will not tell us other people's faults and problems unless He intends us to be part of the solution—either through prayer and intercession or by taking an action on their behalf. So when He does talk to you about someone else's situation, you should be asking Him why He is addressing this with you or how He wants you to be involved in assisting that person.

One day, about a week before Christmas, God spoke to me about the financial difficulties a Christian worker whom I greatly respect was having. He told me she had a low-paying ministry job and that she was struggling and could hardly make ends meet. He told me she did not have any money to buy Christmas presents for her family. Then He told me to do something about it— He told me to give her a hundred dollars so she could buy Christmas presents for her sons. He also gave me a prophetic word of encouragement for her. Yes, it is true that God told me she was in financial hardship. But He only did so because He wanted me to be part of the solution, to give her some money that He desired her to have. He would not have said anything to me about her if He was not going to ask me to assist by giving her the money in His name.

Another time God told me about a person's secret sin

and the thing that had driven that person into the sin. I was really quite surprised—He does not frequently do this with me. At the time I was using the Internet to participate in a Christian chat room. Someone sent me a private message in response to something I'd shared in the room. We started to chat privately.

After a bit, she said, "You'd hate and detest me if you knew what I was really like." Right then God whispered to me, "She is a lesbian." She assumed that all believers hate gay people and want to see them destroyed instead of loving them and wanting to see them saved and healed.

So I said to her, "Why do you think that I will hate you just because you are gay?"

"How did you know I was gay?" she replied. "Who told you?"

I replied, "God did."

She was stunned, and after a bit she said, "I guess God must really hate me, huh?"

At that moment God showed me precisely how He wanted to minister to her. So I said, "No, He loves you very much." Then I proceeded to apologize to her for the way Christians have misrepresented God to the gay community as Someone who hates them and wants to destroy them. I explained that in reality He is Someone who loves them and wants to save them. I told her God knew about all her pain and wanted to heal her and give her His joy and peace. Then I asked her to please forgive me, as a member of the Christian community, for having allowed God to be misrepresented to her like that.

She broke down and started crying. God was touching her heart. Then God began to tell me a lot of details of her life, about her younger brother whom her parents felt could do no wrong, while she could do nothing right. God told me how she was blamed for everything that went wrong, regardless of whose fault it really was. He showed me the pain and the rejection that she had been through. I shared all of this with her, telling her that God knew exactly who she was and that He loved her. I explained that He was reaching out to her with His arms of love. Would she take His hand and accept Jesus as her Savior?

She did. She left the gay lifestyle almost immediately after that as God began to transform her heart. Shortly after that she gave up drugs and began to walk in the Lord's victory in many areas of her life.

The reason God told me her secret sin was because He wanted to use me to minister to it so He could turn her life around. Otherwise God would not have mentioned it to me. God is not going to tell you other people's dirt just so you can know about it. And He is not going to tell other people your dirt. He is not like that. God is not a gossip.

GOD'S VOICE IS NOT
THE VOICE OF CONDEMNATION

The enemy is quick to condemn us. Our own hearts are also quick to condemn us. But the Bible says clearly, "Therefore, there is now no condemnation for those who are in Christ Jesus, because through Christ Jesus the law of the Spirit of life set me free from the law of sin and death" (Rom. 8:1–2, NIV). The paraphrase of these verses is, "God won't ever condemn me because of what Jesus did for me on Calvary."

Does that mean that the Holy Spirit won't ever convict us if we need it? Of course not. *Conviction* and *condemnation* are not the same thing. Let's look at the differences.

Conviction encourages us; it gives us a solution to a

specific problem. Conviction is designed to move us toward God, to get us doing things His way so that we can be in right relationship with Him. Condemnation is designed to push us away from God, to separate us from Him.

Condemnation is vague and abstract. It says, "You are not OK." Conviction is specific. It says, "This behavior you are doing is wrong. It separates you from God." Condemnation discourages and breeds hopelessness. It presents the picture that nothing can ever fix this problem. The end goal of condemnation is to make us give up. The end goal of conviction is to help us reach our maximum potential, to be all we can be in Christ.

There are times when we need correcting. When we need it, God corrects us. Just as any loving father corrects his children for their own good, so God our heavenly Father corrects us. God's correction is not punishment; it is helping us fix a problem so that we can be closer to Him.

There have been times—some recent—when God has corrected me. One time I continued to worry and fret about something that God had already told me He had taken care of. So God said to me, "Teresa, child, I am not angry with you. But I find Myself telling you this again and again. Why are you so hesitant in your heart to believe Me?"

I knew I was being corrected, but there was still much warmth in His voice. I said to Him, "Lord, I'm being rebuked, aren't I?"

He replied, "Yes, child, you are—in love, with much affection. It is not My desire to see you in torment like this. That is why I am correcting you, that you might have My peace."

I am so glad that when He corrects us, God does not

117

condemn us and push us away. About two years ago, my husband, Ed, and I had a rather strong disagreement. We don't disagree often—thank God! We both were unkind and said things designed to hurt the other's feelings. Later I felt guilty and sinful about what I had said to my husband, and I was hurt by what he said to me.

When it was time for my evening devotions, guess what? I did not want to get near God while I felt so sinful and dirty. I knew that God would speak to me when I went to bed (He always does), so I found a "solution." I stayed up all night watching TV, finally falling asleep on the sofa in some awkward position that gave me a kink in my neck. The next morning I awoke late (still on the sofa) and had to rush to get ready for work, conveniently avoiding my morning devotions with God. It was a miserable day.

I am used to having God meet me many times during the day, but this day He did not meet me once. I really began to miss Him. By the end of the day I wanted to be "right with God," no matter what His terms and conditions were. When I got home from work, I told Him so. God told me, "Get paper and pencil and write." (He sometimes tells me that when He wants to speak to me.) Usually what God says in times like this is very private, but I feel that He wants me to share this communication with you:

> Welcome, daughter; come into My presence. You should not have allowed the incident to push you away from My presence. Now come back to Me and find My blessings, for they are surely upon you. Now, Teresa, who moved? Did I pull away from you? Or did you pull away from Me?

I had to confess that I was the one who had moved. Then God continued.

> Well, guess what? If I want to withdraw My presence from you for a season, I can certainly do it on My own. I don't need your help! Sweetheart, don't decide to withdraw your presence from Me! It is not good for you. It causes you unnecessary pain and suffering. It is not My way. Never punish yourself by deciding you are too dirty to come to Me. Instead, come to Me and let Me wash and cleanse you. Let Me shine My light on you and dispel any darkness. Let Me shower you in My truth. Teresa, running to Me when you feel dirty is much safer than running away from Me. You cannot survive apart from Me. Don't even consider it. If I wanted you separated from Me, I would separate you. But this is a season of intimacy. Run to Me no matter how dirty you feel.
>
> Run to Me; I am a safe place, and My arms are wide open to embrace you. Run to Me.

What the Lord spoke to me can apply to you, too. When you feel that you have displeased God, or that He is correcting you, don't run from His presence. Run *to* Him—run to His embrace. Run to the safety of His arms.

POINTS TO PONDER

1. Do you think that it is harder for you to hear the Lord's voice clearly when you are tired or exhausted than when you are rested?

2. Have you ever had an experience where you needed to hear from God about something

important, but the situation you needed to hear about made you so anxious that it was harder to hear God's voice? If so, how did you handle that? Did God eventually break through despite the anxiety, or did He help you find peace first and then speak to you about the situation?

3. Have you ever had a time when the Lord seemed to communicate to you in an obscure and hard-to-understand manner? (Was it through a dream, by any chance? Many people have dreams that seem that they are from God, but that also seem obscure and hard to understand.) If God wants to communicate to us clearly, why do you think He communicated to you in this obscure fashion?

   How did you go about processing the information from Him? Did you ask Him for clarity about it? If so, did He give it to you?

4. What do you think about the concept that God is not going to give you private and personal information about others unless you are either a part of the problem or a part of the solution? If God does speak to you about private details of someone else's life, how do you think He wants you to handle it? Are there times where He might want you to share this information with others? If so, what are some examples where He might want you to share this information, and with whom? Are there times where the Lord might not want you to share private information with others?

5. Have you ever experienced self-condemnation or condemnation from the enemy? Have you experienced the conviction of the Holy Spirit? How are these two similar? How are they different?

6. Can you think of a time when the Holy Spirit convicted you without condemning you? What was that like? How did you feel about that experience? How did you react to God?

TEN

Are You a Seer?

When someone communicates with us, we use our five senses to perceive it. We *see* them, *hear* their words, *feel* their touch or *smell* or *taste* something. We process the inputs that come in through these five senses and assign meanings and perceptions to them—and *communication* occurs.

Generally this communication process works very well, but it is not always perfect. It is possible for a person to intend to communicate one thing, but the one who receives the communication may attach a totally different meaning to it. This happens because the communicator must translate his or her thoughts into something the receiver can perceive through the five senses. The message is transmitted through words, facial expressions, tone of voice and gestures. The receiver hears the words and sees the gestures, and he receives the message through his senses. The receiver then translates what he has seen, heard and felt into a message. He assigns a meaning to it, and communication has occurred.

God gave us precisely five senses for this communication process. It was not an accident—He specifically created humanity with these five senses. These are the mechanisms God gave to us to receive input from the world. We use them constantly to communicate with one another.

In the same way, God specifically designed and created us to be able to communicate with Him. The parallelism is evident—just as God designed us to be able to communicate with each other, so He designed us to be able to communicate with Him. When God communicates to us, He frequently does so in a manner that utilizes one or more of the five senses with which He created us.

In order for us to better understand how God communicates with us, let's take a closer look at the sensory methods He uses. For simplicity, I want to categorize the five senses into three categories—Seeing, Hearing and Sensing (including smell, taste and touch). God may communicate through only one of these categories, or He may use all three to communicate with you. God may show you something, speak to you about its meaning at the same time and give you a sense or physical sensation regarding it. The apostle John experienced this in the Book of Revelation.

In Revelation 10 John received a very in-depth communication from God that involved at least four of his five senses.

Let's look at how God uses each of the three categories mentioned above in this vision to John.

1. *Seeing*—In verses 1–2 and 5, John saw the angels.

He was able to give details about what each angel looked like, what he wore, what he was holding and gestures he made.

2. *Hearing*—In verses 3–4, 6–8 and 11, we find the sense of hearing in operation. Both angels speak and make proclamations, and John heard them. In fact, John described the sound of one angel's voice (vv. 3–4). John also repeated the words that the angels spoke (vv. 6–8, 11).

3. *Sensing*—In verse 10, we see the sense of taste ("it tasted as sweet as honey in my mouth"). The sense of touch (physical feelings) can also be seen in verse 10, because the scroll turned his stomach sour, or gave him a bellyache.

In just this one small portion of John's prophetic vision we see that God used several means to communicate His message to John. John *heard* from God in a manner that used four of his five senses all at the same time.

There are times when God talks to us primarily through just one sense. At other times He combines many senses in a single communication. The Lord will sometimes use multiple senses when He communicates with us. God does not have to use all the sensory mechanisms, but He may.

When you first begin to receive communications from God, He may start you with one sensory category. But as your ability to hear Him matures, He may add additional ways of communicating. So, as an example, if you are not a seer today, God may later begin to give you pictures in addition to the primary method He is currently using to communicate with you.

124

WHAT IS A SEER?

A *seer* is someone with whom God communicates through pictures. A picture, or image, from God can take different forms. God may give you a vision that you see with your physical eyes. Sometimes a vision from God must be seen with opened eyes. At other times you may receive a vision from God that can only be seen with closed eyes. Or perhaps you will be able to see the picture whether your eyes are opened or closed.

Most of the time, people do not see pictures from God with their physical eyes. They see the pictures as flashes in their minds, in a way very similar to closing your eyes and trying to remember a familiar object. As you do that, you create a mental picture, or an image, in your mind, drawn from your own memory. The pictures God gives may look very similar to our own mental pictures or images—except that the source is God instead of our memory.

Not long ago I attended a seminar where the attendees performed an exercise that illustrates this concept. The instructor asked everyone to close their eyes and picture their best friends' faces. Then he asked everyone who'd seen anything that looked like their friend to raise their hand. Most of the hands in the room went up. Then he began to ask a few questions that forced us to think about how we had perceived the pictures of our friends: Were the images in color or black and white? Did the image flash before our eyes, or did it stay there for a long time?

I decided to visualize my husband's face for that exercise. When I closed my eyes and *saw* him, I did not see what looked like a photograph of Ed. First I saw his hair and how it tufts a certain way. Then I saw his eyes—very blue and crystal clear. Then I saw his nose, and finally his smile. Had I seen a picture of Ed, recalled from my memory? Yes, I had.

It was an *accurate* picture, but it was not a *complete* picture. He has aspects that I did not see—such as his forehead, cheeks, chin and ears. There are many parts of Ed that were not seen in this mental picture. Yet I was able to recognize the image as my husband.

I learned something interesting about how I visualize things from this exercise. Visualization is not my strongest point. I don't tend to think in images, and when I do they are not always complete.

So, it is not surprising that when God first started speaking to me, He did not use a lot of pictures to do so. Those came later on after my hearing had improved substantially. On the other hand, if you are a visual person, then pictures may be the first way God speaks to you. But again, there are no guarantees. Hearing God is not a formula or recipe we follow. It is a process requiring that we build a relationship with Him. He takes each of us through a slightly different process in learning to hear and discern His voice.

IMAGES FROM GOD

The images we receive from God may be in color, or they may be in black and white. They may be a *still shot*, like a photograph, or they may be in motion, like a movie. You may see them in their entirety, as if someone were holding a photograph before your face. Or you may see them in pieces, as I did when I visualized Ed's face in the earlier exercise. The image may begin as a close-up, and then the picture may pan back over a larger image to give you a context. You may receive a

ARE YOU A SEER?

broad-based picture that seems to zoom in on a specific detail, explicitly calling that detail to your attention. You might see the picture superimposed over a real scene at which you are looking in the natural. For instance, one time as I watched a man who was preaching in my church, I could see the podium, the platform and the walls behind him. Suddenly I saw a picture superimposed over the "screen"—the area of my vision—at which I was looking. The same man was standing there, but the background changed. I still saw the real background of our church, but I could also distinctly see another background. This background I recognized to be the platform of a Christian convention center, a huge auditorium that seats several thousand people. It was like a double-exposure picture. Both the real image and the supernatural image could be seen.

I understood the picture to be God telling me that this man would be invited to speak at a large conference. I shared the picture with the speaker. About six months later, the fulfillment of that picture happened for him.

As another example, I attended a class at Fuller Seminary where Cindy Jacobs (the founder and head of Generals of Intercession) was in our class. Although she was a student, on one afternoon she taught the class. That day I sat only two seats away from her on the front row. I had never heard of her before the class, but it soon became apparent to me that she was a very powerful and anointed intercessor.

Three months later, I visited a prayer group for women at an inner-city church. I had talked to one of the leaders of the group on the phone before I came. When I met this particular leader in person, I was amazed at how much she looked like Cindy Jacobs. When she prayed, it was very clear to me that she knew how to hear God. I perceived that she was a very effective intercessor. I was struck by the similarity of her anointing to Cindy's anointing, and at how much she resembled Cindy in physical appearance.

However, at the end of the evening I took another good, hard look at this leader, and I realized that she did not look much like Cindy at all. I could not imagine why I had thought she looked like Cindy. So I asked the Lord about it. He told me that I had been seeing her anointing in the form of Cindy's image. He explained that He had superimposed the face of someone I knew (Cindy) over another person's face to show me they had a similar anointing. It is a communication method He uses frequently with me when He wants to show me the anointing on someone's life.

When God shows you a picture, it may happen very quickly, flashing before your "mind's eyes," then fading and leaving you only a memory of the picture. Do not discount a picture from God if He shows it to you quickly. He sometimes does it that way. Usually when God shows me a picture, it goes away almost instantly, but I can remember it in great detail.

On the other hand, some people find that the picture stays before them for several minutes, allowing them time to take a good, long look at it to note specific details. Some people forget the picture shortly after seeing it. Others can recall it for a long time.

I have a friend to whom God frequently gives pictures. After she sees the picture, she has a mental *filing box* into which she puts it. Any time she wants to look at a picture again, she can recall any picture that God has ever shown her. The clarity of the picture, and its duration, will vary from person to person.

Pictures are good, because they communicate many

details rapidly. You have, no doubt, heard the idiom that "a picture is worth a thousand words." This is very true. A picture allows you very quickly and precisely to communicate a lot of information. It would take four or five pages to describe my house. I would need to give great details—what color it is, the style of building, what the yard and fence look like, where the windows are located, the type of tiles on the roof, its proximity to other houses, the general condition of the exterior and other details. Or I could get my Polaroid camera, take a photograph and hand it to you.

You would probably get a much more precise perception of my house from the photo than from description four to five pages long. You could process information from the photo in less time than it would take you to read the essay. Pictures are a good way to communicate a lot of detail in a short amount of time.

But the problem with pictures is that you don't always understand what they mean. Let's take an example. Pretend that I just handed you a photograph of an elderly man sitting in a wheel chair. Would you, from this photo alone, understand what I was trying to communicate? There would be many different assumptions that you could make and many different details on which you might focus.

You might see the bleakness of the convalescent hospital around him, the details of the age lines in his face or the color and pattern of the afghan covering his lap. You might notice the color of his hair and eyes or the wrinkles in his hands. But what would that picture communicate to you?

Would you assume it was a photo of my father or grandfather? Would you think I work at a retirement home? Would you think that I desire to minister to this sad-looking man? Or would you think that I have a ministry of knitting afghans and giving them to the elderly? Would you think that I was in the business of running a retirement home or maybe that I was a wheelchair salesman? Perhaps I was trying to collect donations to help care for the elderly. From that picture alone you really can't determine the meaning and message I wanted to communicate to you.

Sometimes it is like that with pictures from the Lord. You can see a lot of details. You can gather a lot of information. But you may not understand what it means and why God is showing it to you.

Not all pictures are like that. Sometimes the picture is very clear, and you can easily draw the meaning from the context of the situation for which God gave you that picture. For instance, pretend you have misplaced your keys and spent ten minutes looking for them—to no avail. You stop and ask God where they are. Suddenly you see a picture of them sitting on the coffee table covered by a *Charisma* magazine. You would understand precisely what that picture means, wouldn't you? It means that you should go to the coffee table, pick up the magazine and retrieve your keys from under it. In this case, God has communicated very clearly and precisely through a picture.

There are times when you will get an image without an explanation. You will wonder how to handle this partial revelation. The solution is actually pretty simple. Just remember this: If God shows you a picture or image, then He must have something He wants to communicate to you. If you don't understand His communication, then go back to Him and ask Him. God's goal is to communicate with you. He knows how to make the explanation clear to you.

We can see how He did this in the record of His commissioning of Jeremiah. When God first communicated to Jeremiah that He was appointing him as a prophet to the nations, Jeremiah protested, "Ah, Lord GOD! Behold, I cannot speak, for I am a youth" (Jer. 1:6). In essence he was telling God that he did not understand how to prophesy, that in fact he was too young to do so.

In response, God encouraged him by telling Jeremiah that He would be with him (v. 8). Then He showed Jeremiah a picture of a branch of an almond tree (v. 11). When Jeremiah did not understand the picture, God explained it to him (v. 12).

Then God showed him another picture that Jeremiah did not understand (v. 13). This picture was of a pot of boiling liquid that was facing away from the north. God explained the picture to Jeremiah (vv. 14–19). God concluded His explanation by once again confirming to Jeremiah, "I am with you…to deliver you" (v. 19). That was enough! Suddenly this young and inexperienced prophet had a powerful word from God for rebellious Judah.

HOW GOD COMMUNICATES
THE MEANING OF PICTURES

So, how does God communicate the meaning of a picture to us when we ask Him for clarity or understanding? He can do it in any number of ways. Sometimes He will do it pictorially by changing the image itself. Perhaps when you see a picture of a huge crowd, you ask God for the meaning. Suddenly the image changes, zooming in on one individual. You look at the individual more closely, and realize it is you. You become aware that God is paying personal attention to you. You realize that He cares about you, and you are important to Him. He has, as it were, chosen you out of the crowd to let you know just how precious you are to Him.

Sometimes God will give further information to you when you ask Him for it. Perhaps you see a picture of a close friend driving, with his entire family in his car. The car is stopped at a stop sign, and he is waiting to turn left. Because you have no idea what that picture means, you ask God for clarification.

Suddenly the picture changes, and you see a large truck barreling at full speed toward your friend's car, about to rear-end them. A sense of danger and urgency wells up in your spirit. Immediately you begin to pray and intercede for your friend's protection. After ten minutes or so, the urgency leaves you, and you no longer feel impressed to intercede.

In a case like this, God uses several different sensory mechanisms to communicate to you. Through the picture He shows you—*seeing*—that your friend is in danger. You *sensed* (we will discuss *sensing* in chapter 12) the urgency and the leading of the Holy Spirit to intercede for your friend, and you instantly obeyed. In this case, God started with a picture to get your attention and then used various means to give you a more complete understanding and plan of action.

Sometimes God will give you a whole story or a complex meaning in a single image. Then when He shows you the picture, it is like shorthand for something that would take a long time to communicate if the understanding were not already in place. Communications like these usually come from our own past experiences.

OTHER "SEEING" EXPERIENCES FOR A SEER

Seers are not limited simply to getting pictures or images. Sometimes God will focus your attention, or fix your gaze, on something. Even when you try to focus on something else, your gaze keeps being drawn back to this object. It is almost as if you were a camera with a zoom lens, and God has zoomed you in on something specific. Your attention is riveted to that one image.

It may be that the Lord has glued your eyes upon someone, and you simply cannot stop looking at that person. Or perhaps He fixes your attention on an object. When God does this, He has a reason for doing so. The best strategy is to ask God why He is focusing your attention on this thing and what He wants you to do regarding it.

Let me share an example. I have a friend who, in her late thirties, was still single—and she felt very self-conscious about being single. She was very sweet and very attractive, but no one ever seemed to ask her out. Finally, one man began to date her. They were about as opposite as two people could be. She was short and petite. He was tall and overweight. She was quiet and sophisticated. He was loud, coarse and uneducated.

For a while things went along OK, but then he asked her to marry him. She was in a state of crisis over this. She had only dated him because she did not want to be alone. They were so different that she was not sure she wanted to spend the rest of her life with him. On the other hand, not having a boyfriend made her feel badly about herself. She thought that anyone her age who was still single must not be OK.

She asked me to meet her for lunch to pray with her

133

and help her sort this out. She wanted to know if God wanted her to marry this man. When we met, she was wearing a bright purple blouse, and the Lord kept calling my attention to it. She is an attractive girl, and pleasant to look at, and I tried to look at her face as we talked. But my gaze kept being drawn to her shoulder. All I could see was a sea of purple before my eyes. I would try to force myself to look in her eyes, but seconds later my focus was back on her shoulder.

Finally I prayed and asked God about it. I wanted God to help me concentrate on her, and all I could seem to focus on was her purple shirt. God responded by asking me, "Teresa, what does the color purple mean?"

I had studied the prophetic symbolism of colors, so I knew the answer to that. "It is the majesty of God," I replied silently.

"OK," God said, "tell her that."

It seemed like an odd request, but I have learned to obey. So I said to her, "The Lord told me to tell you that you are clothed in the majesty of God."

She broke down and started crying. I did not understand her reaction until she explained it to me. The previous night when she had been praying and seeking God, He kept telling her that she did not need to obtain her sense of value through being someone's girlfriend or wife. He kept telling her that He had personally clothed her in His majesty, and that is where she would get her sense of worth. I did not know anything about what God had said to her, but the words about being clothed in the majesty of God were a strong confirmation of what God had already spoken to her. She knew she had indeed heard Him the night before, and that she did not need to marry this man whom she did not love.

God had focused my attention on something purple

to get me to tell her that she was clothed in the majesty of God. Sometimes He will do that with us. When He wants us to pay attention to something specific, He will keep drawing our attention to it until we begin to seek Him for more direction about what He is showing us.

Sometimes God uses other visual means to speak to a seer. It is not uncommon at all for God to speak to a seer through movies, pictures, in magazine articles and even cartoons. God will focus a seer's attention on something in a movie and begin to speak to the seer through it. For instance, many seers have gone to a secular movie, such as *The Lion King* or *Braveheart*, and come away feeling the movie was prophetic because God spoke to them during it.

SCRIPTURAL PRECEDENT FOR SEERS

Scripture gives many examples of God's communication with seers. The Major and Minor Prophets, as well as 1 Samuel through 2 Chronicles, are filled with many examples.

The prophet Amos was very much a seer. In Amos 7:1–2 he had a vision of locusts destroying Israel. That vision resulted in powerful intercession by Amos (vv. 2–3). He had another vision in verse 4 of God destroying Israel by fire. Again he interceded (vv. 5–6), and God's judgment was turned away. In verses 7–9 he had another vision, this time of a plumb line. In Amos 8:1–3 he had a vision of a bowl of summer fruit. He did not understand the meaning of this vision at first, so God gave him the interpretation. Through these examples, we see several incidents in Amos's life where God used pictures to communicate with him.

Let's look at a New Testament example. In Acts 10, the Lord communicated with Peter and Cornelius through pictures. In verses 1–6, Cornelius saw angels in a vision and was given instructions to send for Peter. God also spoke to Peter in a vision, but Peter did not understand the vision (vv. 9–17). However, he did have enough understanding to know God wanted him to go to Cornelius's house when he was invited, which was a violation of the Jewish etiquette with which he'd been raised. He did not get a full understanding of the vision until God poured out His Holy Spirit on Cornelius and his household in Acts 10:28.

The account of the apostle Paul's vision of Ananias is a powerful scriptural example of receiving a picture from God that was clearly a mental picture—not something seen with physical eyes. Jesus met Paul (then known as Saul) on the road to Damascus in a divine manifestation of blinding light. Saul fell to the ground, and Jesus spoke to him. The people traveling with Saul heard God's voice but did not see anything. When Saul got up off the ground, he was blind (Acts 9:8). But although he could not see anything with his physical eyes, blind Saul sees Ananias praying for him to receive his sight (vv. 11–12).

There are many other biblical precedents for God speaking to people through pictures or images. I believe this is a very common way God communicates with His children today. A lot of people are visual and tend to think in pictures, so it is not at all surprising God uses pictures (and other visual means) to interact with us.

Remember, God's main interest is to communicate with us. He wants us to "hear Him" or see what He is trying to show us. Pictures are a nice, concrete way for

Him to get our attention. When we see a picture, we know that God is showing us something. But the downside of pictures is that we may not always immediately understand what God means to communicate with that picture. If that happens, then consider the picture as a personal invitation to come to the Lord and dialogue with Him about what He just showed you. If you ask Him for wisdom (or an understanding of what He wants to show you), then He will give it to you (James 1:5).

POINTS TO PONDER

1. Have you ever received a picture or image that you believe is from the Lord? Did you understand its meaning immediately, or did you have to seek God for it? Was it a picture in your mind's eye, or was it a vision that you saw with your eyes open? How long did the picture stay before you? Was it very quick, or did it last for a while?

2. How frequently does God speak to you through pictures? How do you respond to Him when He does?

3. How would you go about gaining understanding of a picture God has shown that you do not immediately understand?

4. Has the Lord ever drawn your attention to something or fixed your gaze on someone? If so, how long did it take you to figure out that God was trying to show you something? Was it immediate, or did it take a while? How did the understanding dawn on you?

5. This chapter shared a few examples from Scripture of God's speaking to His children through pictures. Can you think of any more references or examples of this in the Bible?

ELEVEN

Are You a Hearer?

A hearer is someone who hears what God is saying to him or her. God communicates with a hearer using language—words and sentences. His voice is seldom audible. We don't usually hear it with our physical ears; instead we hear Him in our thoughts. We usually describe this type of communication as God's "still small voice" (1 Kings 19:12).

When we communicate via language, we use words and sentences to express thoughts and meaning. The words are often spoken and heard. When people speak, they first form ideas in the mind that they wish to communicate. Then they select words and sentences to transmit the ideas. In this way, speaking starts in the mind and then goes out through the vocal cords. The vocal cords produce vibrations or sound waves, which travel through the air to the person who is "listening" to them.

When we listen (or hear), our ear "catches" the sound waves and directs them to our eardrums. The eardrums convert the physical sound waves back into words and sentences in our mind. We do not understand the words with our physical ears; our ears simply convert sound waves into thoughts. Our mind processes the thoughts and attaches meaning and understanding to those words. In reality, when we "hear," the understanding takes place in our *mind*, not in our *ear*. The physical ears are important in hearing because they "catch" the sound waves and translate them into thoughts. But the real "hearing" takes place in our brain.

When God wants to communicate with us, He uses much the same process, except He bypasses our physical ears. God decides that He has something to say to us. He chooses words and sentences to express that idea to us. Then He drops those words directly into our mind. At that point, they sound very similar to our own thoughts, except that they originate from God instead of from us.

Let me prove to you that you don't need your physical ears to "hear" something. Finish reading this paragraph. Then think your first and last name silently to yourself. If you were me, you would think, *Teresa Seputis*. But you are not me, so please use your own name instead of mine. (OK, stop reading now and think your name.)

Did you hear your name as you thought it? That was the voice of your own thoughts. Your physical ears were not engaged, but you "heard" something, didn't you? You heard it because most of the "hearing" takes place in our thoughts, not in our ears. Try it again. This time silently "say" the month and date of your birthday. Mine is "November 4." Go ahead and silently "say" yours.

Did you hear it again? It sounded pretty similar to the way your name sounded, didn't it? It may or may not have been identical, but it will have been pretty similar. Now you are getting an idea of what the voice of your own thoughts sounds like. Here is the catch—when God bypasses our physical ears and drops His words and sentences into our minds, it sounds the same as the voice of our own thoughts. God's still, small voice sounds just like our own thoughts.

This has its advantages and its disadvantages. The advantage is that it is a nice, clear way to communicate. It is easy to understand. The disadvantage is that it sounds so much like our own thoughts that sometimes we are not sure when it is God and when it is ourselves. In fact, that similarity works very much against us, because sometimes we will not realize that we are hearing God, and we will ignore Him. The similarity can tend to cause us to discount God's voice.

There are times when God speaks to us, and we ignore Him. We don't do this intentionally. We do it because we confuse His voice with our own thoughts. We discount what we believe to be our own thoughts. As a result, God can speak to us and we may not realize He is doing so. We might "miss it" and go away feeling frustrated. We need to know how to sort out when it is God speaking to us and when it is just our own thinking.

LEARNING TO RECOGNIZE GOD'S VOICE

The first step in the process is that we must consider that what sounds like our own thoughts might actually be God. We have to listen to them so that we can judge and evaluate them. Many people find this uncomfortable because they desire to be led only by God's Spirit and not by their own imagination. They do not want to mistake their own ideas and desires for God's voice, so they try to disregard all their own thoughts and listen only for God. But if you block out your own thoughts, you will probably block out God's voice as well. As you practice listening to God, it will become easier to discern when it is He and when it is just your own thoughts. At some point you will be able to tell the difference between the two quickly, easily and with a fair degree of accuracy.

It's simple but true: The only way to hear God is to start listening. Evaluate everything you hear. Run the words through the filter of Scripture. If it does not line up with Scripture, then discount it. If it passes that filter, take it to God and tell Him what you heard. Ask Him if He was really saying those things to you. Ask Him to confirm the message for you, and to correct it and clarify it because you want to know only His voice. He is very faithful. He will be happy to work with you in this process.

You might feel what I call a "confirmation in your spirit." That is a deep certainty from within the very depths of your being that encourages you in knowing that was God's voice. Or perhaps God will use natural means to confirm that you heard Him. He might give you some confirmations through circumstances to indicate that you heard clearly. Or He might increase your understanding in an area so you can evaluate what you heard Him say. And if you heard "wrong," God might put a "check in you spirit" about what you heard. In other words, something might rise up inside of you that says, "No, that was not God."

God is incredibly faithful and reliable. He will not allow you to fall into fallacy when you sincerely seek

Him with a heart to obey. Even if you hear wrongly, and act upon what you heard, God will lovingly correct you and steer you back to the right path. You can depend on Him to do that because He is absolutely dependable. He promised that He would not give us evil when we ask Him for good things—like hearing His voice clearly (Matt. 7:7–11).

Don't expect 100 percent accuracy when you begin. As with so many things, there's a learning curve to hearing from God. Children don't go directly from counting to ten to solving calculus problems. There are many learning steps in between—like multiplication, algebra and trigonometry. Likewise, there will be steps that the Holy Spirit will cause you to take as you learn to discern God's voice.

When I first started hearing God speak to me in that still, small voice, I was only about 50 percent accurate. That means that I misheard about half of the time. But the other half of the time *I really heard God!* I could have become discouraged about the times I heard wrong and considered giving up. But instead, I got excited about the times that God really spoke to me, and I heard Him! That drove me to press in for more. Over time, my accuracy kept improving. I am still not at 100 percent in distinguishing God's "still small voice" from my own thoughts, but I am a whole lot closer than I used to be. Likewise, your accuracy and clarity of hearing will improve as you keep listening to God and keep practicing hearing Him.

God seems to enjoy using the "still small voice" to speak to us about intimate situations, such as in prayer, devotions and worship time. He may also use that method to give us specific instructions or show us how to do something. For example, one night as I drove home late, I was about to pull off the freeway to get gas. Suddenly God said, "Teresa, don't get off here. Stay on the freeway." I obeyed Him, but I asked Him why. The Lord replied, "Because the gas station is closed." The next time I filled up, I checked their hours, and sure enough, they were closed at the time God told me not to get gas.

God has a "chatty" personality. He enjoys talking to us just as we enjoy talking to our children. He also likes to give us what I call "confidence-building exercises." In this way, God sets us up for success. A confidence-building exercise happens when He tells us something and then confirms that word to us almost immediately. In this way He gives us clear and easily observable feedback on our hearing. He often does this in small everyday life things. They are real confidence boosters, letting us know we are really hearing Him.

God often does this with me by speaking to me as I drive. As I approach a red light, God often tells me whether or not it will turn green before I come to a complete stop. At first I could not figure out why God would talk to me about something as insignificant as traffic lights. But as He talked to me about the traffic lights—and I heard Him clearly—I realized that *every time* He said a light would turn green, it did, and I did not have to come to a complete stop. Every time He said it would stay red until I stopped, it did.

Soon He began talking to me about traffic patterns during rush hour. He would tell me which lane to get in and when to change lanes. As a result, I always ended up in the "right" lane, the one that was moving. I would get through the traffic snarl much more quickly than everyone else. (I enjoyed those lessons! They were very practical.)

God also began to tell me how many minutes I would have to wait for my subway train to arrive. God did this for about three months. Then finally He explained why He was doing it—He wanted to give me success opportunities in hearing Him so I would be more confident in my hearing of His voice.

Gradually, God "upped the stakes" a little. He began speaking about more significant things, but still things I could confirm. One time He told me that a coworker was very concerned about her teenager, who was making dangerous mistakes and bad choices. A few minutes after God spoke, I saw the coworker in the lunchroom. I didn't really know her personally, but since God had spoken to me about her, I struck up a conversation. In the conversation I asked if she had any kids. Shortly after my question, she began sharing about her troublesome teen. I discovered that she was also a Christian, and I was able to pray with her about the situation. She told me she had been sitting there praying about her child when I came up to her. It was a real encouragement to her that God was listening to her prayers.

God had spoken to me about something more significant than traffic lights—and not only did I get a confirmation, but I also got to minister to a sister and make a new friend.

God loves to orchestrate confidence-building exercises so that we can know we really are hearing Him. He also enjoys giving us simple and direct commands and watching us obey Him. I have learned that God seldom explains to me why He is asking me to do something. He just gives the command and expects me to obey Him.

When we obey, God often sends an opportunity to minister or to receive a blessing, but not always. Let me share one of my favorite examples. I love cut flowers, but my husband seldom buys them for me. One day I was working at my desk on the eighth floor of a skyscraper. Suddenly God told me to go downstairs "right now" and go outside. I did not want to stop what I was doing, but God repeated Himself, so I obeyed. When I got to the building lobby and opened the door, a lady walked by carrying the most beautiful bouquet I had ever seen. My glance must have been more obvious than I realized, because she stopped and handed me the flowers. She explained that she was mad at the man who gave them to her and was about to throw them away. Since I obviously liked them, she'd rather I have them. I said thank you, and she walked away. Then I asked God what He wanted me to do next. He replied, "You can go back to work now. I sent you outside because I wanted to give you those flowers." If I had not obeyed Him, I would have missed a blessing.

OTHER METHODS GOD USES

There are many other ways that "hearers" hear God. Let's look at some.

SPEAKING THROUGH INTENSELY FOCUSED THOUGHTS

Sometimes we can hear God through intensely focused thoughts, which often arise out of prayer, about a specific issue. Let me illustrate with an example. When I sat down to write this book, I expected this chapter to be the easiest to write because I teach on it frequently. But it actually turned out to be one of the hardest. I wrote it and did not like the way it turned out. I threw it away and started over from scratch. My second attempt still did not turn out very good. I spent hours editing it, doctoring it up and trying to make it work. But I was not at all happy with it.

By that time I had already spent four days working on it, and I still did not have anything I liked. One morning while showering, I asked God to please help me write the chapter His way. I said, "Please let it be clear, understandable and interesting." An intensity came over me, and I found myself deep in thought. The Holy Spirit was directing my thinking, but I did not realize it at first.

I began to realize my problem was that I was too knowledgeable on this subject. I knew too much, and I wanted to share it all. Every time I addressed a concept, I went down two or three "rabbit trails" trying to explain underlying principles. I was attempting to pack too much into the chapter.

My thinking was very intense, but I was also aware of the Lord's presence. I invited God into my thinking process, and He said, "Teresa, I am already in it."

"OK, Lord," I said, and went back to my thinking. Then I began to get an outline for this chapter that seemed really good. I got out of the shower, wrapped myself in a towel, went to the computer and wrote down the outline. Later I developed the outline into the text of this chapter. This incident illustrates how God comes, at times, into the intense thinking of a hearer and directs our thoughts.

RECALLING SOMETHING TO OUR MEMORY

God often speaks to a hearer by recalling memories into that person's thinking. You may suddenly find yourself remembering things with great depth and clarity. It may be a phrase, verse of Scripture, song or something someone said to you. The memory seems to apply to some issue about which you are currently seeking God's voice. Although you know it is a memory, it almost seems as if God is telling this to you in response to your current situation. He probably is. He likes to do that.

Let me share an example. I recently ordered cassette tapes from a four-part sermon series that my pastor preached. He had given me permission to have them transcribed and to use them as a teaching series for an Internet class. I listened to all four of the tapes before giving them to the transcriber. The first few sentences on each tape were missing, almost as if the person recording had been caught by surprise and started the tape a bit late. As I thought about that, I wondered why the person in the sound booth would make the same mistake four weeks in a row. Wasn't he paying attention?

Suddenly I strongly remembered when I taught my prophecy class about using hand-held tape recorders when delivering a prophetic word to someone. I told them that cassette tapes have a "lead," usually white or transparent, that does not record. I asked them to be careful to position the tapes past the lead before putting them in the recorder, so that the beginning of the prophecy would not be cut off.

This memory gave me understanding of what had happened with the tape series, and I made a mental note to tell the sound person about winding the tape past the non-recording lead. God had brought back a memory to communicate something to me.

He enjoys recalling things to our memory. When He does this, the memory frequently comes with a greater level of detail or clarity than normal. For instance, He may recall a song to your memory that you have not heard in ten years, but you are able to remember the melody, the chorus and even all the lyrics to the verses.

The Holy Spirit considers helping us to remember things to be a part of His job description. John 14:26 says, "But the Counselor, the Holy Spirit, whom the Father will send in my name, will teach you all things and will remind you of everything I have said to you" (NIV).

BRINGING SCRIPTURE TO OUR MEMORY

God loves to speak to a hearer through Scripture. He will draw us to certain portions of Scripture or will cause us to recall passages from His Word. The scriptures He brings to our recall will address a situation in our lives about which He wants to talk to us.

I was in India on a missions trip in November and December of 1996. About four days before we started home, I received notice that my father had died unexpectedly of a heart attack. My mother wanted me to come home immediately for the funeral. I was in a very rural village. It would take a fourteen-hour train ride to reach the airport. Because I did not speak the local language, it would have been impossible for me to negotiate the train ride, which involved two complicated transfers.

The missions team had only one interpreter. They could not send him with me because they needed him for more ministry and outreach activities. So they decided to send me by taxi directly to the airport. It would be nearly a sixteen-hour drive. I was to begin my trip in five hours, so I packed and then spent some time praying.

As I prayed, the Lord brought two scriptures to my mind. They were not at all the type of scripture I expected Him to give me at a time like this. First I recalled Matthew 10:37, which says, "He who loves

father or mother more than Me is not worthy of Me."
The second verse I recalled stated, "Let the dead bury
their own dead, but you go and preach the kingdom of
God" (Luke 9:60).

Over and over these words ran through my mind.
As I thought about them, I realized that God did not
want me to leave the team and go home ahead of
them. He wanted me to stay and minister. I prayed
about it, and asked God if He gave me those scriptures
to tell me to finish my trip and miss my father's
funeral. He seemed to confirm that plan to me.

Quite frankly, I was a bit shocked that God would
ask me to miss my own father's funeral to do missions
work. It seemed cruel. I thought He was asking a great
deal of me. But I have always known God to be good,
so I obeyed Him. I told the team to cancel the taxi
because God had told me to stay with them.

Four days later we started home by train. During our
trip, the train passed through an area of flatlands that
was very flooded. Many buildings were shoulder deep in
water, and the roads were washed out totally. The ele-
vated train tracks were not affected, but the trip would
have been impossible by car. We asked the conductor
when the flood hit, and were told that it would have
been roughly at the same time as when the taxi would
have been passing through that area if I had gone ahead
of the team. Our interpreter told me that the driver
probably would have dumped me out of the taxi because
he would have considered me to be a "bad omen." He
would have abandoned me (with no money) in a rural
area where no one spoke English. It would have been a
very dangerous situation, possibly a life-threatening one.

That was the reason God told me to stay with the
team. He was not being cruel or harsh; He was pro-

tecting me. When I arrived home, I discovered that my family had been able to postpone the funeral for me, and I was able to attend after all. God took good care of me in this situation. The way He communicated His instructions to me was through Scripture. He frequently speaks to hearers that way.

Bringing songs back to our memory

God likes to recall songs to us, a method He uses often with me. During a class I taught on "How to Hear God's Voice," I was leading the class in an exercise where the students ask God to speak to them, and then they write down what they hear. Mandy*, one of the ladies in the class, had been having a hard time hearing God. Although everyone else in the class was hearing Him clearly, poor Mandy consistently drew a blank. During the first ten minutes of this fifteen-minute exercise, she did not write a single word. Then she bent over her paper and began writing furiously. I could hardly wait to hear what God had spoken to her.

When we began our debriefing time, I asked her to share first. She replied, "Oh, God did not speak to me. I was just remembering some old songs I haven't heard in ages. I decided to jot down parts of the lyrics as I remembered them. It was kind of weird. I'd get one phrase of one song and then a totally different phrase of a different song as I heard the melodies run through my mind. I haven't even read what I wrote down yet."

Her classmates coaxed her to share what she'd written. To our amazement, it was one of the most detailed, beautiful love letters I have ever heard God write to one of His children. It was deeply personal for Mandy, but it also touched and ministered to every one of our hearts as well. The power of God filled that message. I

---

* Not her real name.

will always treasure the look on Mandy's face when she realized that what she had written down was *from God*. She had really heard Him!

God sometimes uses recalled songs to speak to us about really big decisions with major consequences. He did this during my first missions trip to India. As our plane landed in Madras (now Chanai), the pilot announced over the loudspeaker that a major, highly destructive monsoon was rolling in. It was expected to hit land five hours north of Madras.

That was about the time we were scheduled to leave by train. We would pass through that monsoon area on our way to the city in which we were to minister. We were told it would be very dangerous to make the trip.

We met together in the conference room of a hotel to pray and seek direction from God. We began by singing some worship songs. One of them was the words of Revelation 22:17 put into a simple chorus. The gist of the song was, "The Spirit and the bride say, 'Come.'" Worship ended, and we prayed together and sought God. As hard as I tried to focus on the prayer, the words of the chorus kept running through my mind. I could not concentrate. I kept hearing, "The Spirit and the bride say, 'Come'... The Spirit and the bride say, 'Come'... The Spirit and the bride say, 'Come'"... over and over again.

After about forty-five minutes, I finally apologized to God for being so distracted. I confessed to Him that this song kept running through my mind.

Then God asked me, "Teresa, who is the Spirit?"

"The Holy Spirit," I replied.

"And who is the bride?" He asked.

I responded, "The church."

"And what did they say in the song?"

"Lord," I answered, "they said, 'Come.'"

"Well, Teresa," God continued, "did the Holy Spirit tell you to go on this trip?"

"Yes," I responded.

"And did the church in Andhra Pradesh invite you to come and do this outreach?"

"Yes, Lord."

"Then, child," He continued, "you have your answer. Go, just like you were invited. Trust that I will watch over you and keep you safe."

I was the only one on the team who thought they heard directly from God. Seven people put their lives in potential risk on the basis of God's speaking through a song. We got on the train. The storm got behind us and seemed to be chasing our train. It ripped up the train tracks behind us, but it never quite seemed to catch our train. We arrived safely at our destination. In fact, we beat the storm there by about six hours.

The officials came to tell us that we must cancel our meeting because it was illegal to have an outdoor meeting while monsoon warnings were active. We told the officials we would postpone it a few days until the warnings subsided. The officials told us that no one would want to come to our meeting after the monsoon hit. People would be too concerned about losing loved ones and dealing with the destruction of their homes to care about our meetings.

But our interpreter was full of faith as a result of God's speaking through the song and protecting us on the train ride. The Holy Spirit rose up in him, and he told the officials that our God would turn the storm. It would not come into the village. The officials scoffed at this. But the storm approached the city, skirted around the city without entering it and went back out to sea. The officials were amazed. They became our personal publicity agents, telling everyone to go to the meetings and hear about the Christian God who turned the storm away. As a result, many came to the meetings to hear about Jesus, and many were saved.

God had big plans for this trip. He wanted to show forth His glory. Yet He "risked" the plans by communicating His direction to our team through the chorus of a song. God does speak to us in this way, and we must not discount it.

If something seems to be recalling to your memory, and you cannot concentrate on anything else no matter how hard you try, then stop to talk with God about it. It may very well be that He is trying to tell you something.

HEARERS IN GOD'S WORD

There are several examples of hearers in God's Word.

HOSEA

Hosea was a hearer. By reading just the first few verses of the book you will see God speaking (and Hosea hearing Him) over and over again:

- Hosea 1:2—"The LORD said..."
- Hosea 1:4–5—"The LORD said..."
- Hosea 1:6—"God said..."
- Hosea 1:9—"God said..."

MOSES

Moses was not just a hearer, but he frequently dialogued with God. In fact, Moses was so close to God that God said that He "spoke to Moses face to face, as a man speaks to his friend" (Exod. 33:11). God expressed similar feelings about Moses again in Numbers 12:8. Moses first encountered God at the burning bush near

Mount Horeb. The encounter began when God called his name from out of the burning bush (Exod. 3:4). Moses had a prolonged dialogue with God in the following verses.

We can see a pattern emerge for how God communicated to Moses. God spoke, then Moses answered. Then God spoke again, and Moses responded to the further word. In other words, God and Moses held a conversation. The following verses give us a bird's eye view of their conversation:

- God calls; Moses answers—Exodus 3:4
- "He [God] said..."—Exodus 3:5
- "Then He said..."—Exodus 3:6
- "The LORD said..."—Exodus 3:7
- "But Moses said to God..."—Exodus 3:11
- "And He [God] said..."—Exodus 3:12
- "Moses said to God..." (and asks Him for His name)—Exodus 3:13
- "God said to Moses..." (and answers the question)—Exodus 3:14
- "Moreover God said to Moses..."—Exodus 3:15
- "Moses answered..."—Exodus 4:1
- "The LORD said to him...", asking Moses a question to which Moses replied—Exodus 4:2
- "And He [God] said..."—Exodus 4:3
- "Then the LORD said to him..."—Exodus 4:4

The same pattern can be seen in verses 5–17. God says things to Moses; Moses hears Him and responds. They are holding a prolonged conversation.

EZEKIEL

Ezekiel is another example of a hearer who dialogued with God. Here are a few examples:

- "The word of the LORD came to [him]..."—
  Ezekiel 3:16
- "The [Lord]...said to [him]"—Ezekiel 3:22
- "The Spirit...set [him] on [his] feet, and
  spoke with [him] and said..."—Ezekiel 3:24
- Ezekiel dialogues with God and gets a change
  in his instructions—Ezekiel 4:14–15
- "He [God] said..."—Ezekiel 4:16

Again in the example from Ezekiel's life we see a conversation taking place between God and His hearer. Scripture sets a strong precedence for *hearers*.

POINTS TO PONDER

1. Has there ever been a time when God recalled something, like a song, conversation or memory, to your memory? Can you describe the scenario?

2. Has there ever been a time when God spoke to you through Scripture? Please describe the circumstances surrounding this.

3. Have you ever heard God speak to you in that still, small voice? If so, what kinds of things did He discuss with you?

4. Do you find it hard or easy to discern your own thoughts from God's still, small voice? Why do you think that is? How can a person go about making it easier to discern the difference between the two?

TWELVE

Are You a "Senser"?

A "senser" is one who senses that God is communicating supernatural information, insights or direction to him or her through the senses of touch, smell and taste. Along with the sensory message is a sense of "just knowing" or a spiritual "hunch." Suddenly you have information you did not have before. You cannot explain how and why you know what you know, but that information turns out to be precise and accurate regarding something about which you have no natural knowledge. God supernaturally deposits the knowledge in your spirit. One minute you did not know it. The next minute it is there, and you feel confident about it.

Some people call those who hear God in this manner "knower/feelers," a term that I believe was coined by Dr. Bill Hamon, founder and head of Christian International (CI). I have recently stopped using this term because it is not quite broad enough for what this type of divine communication entails. The term "feeler" implies only the sense of touch. But God will also speak to sensers through smell and sometimes even through taste.

Sensing is probably the most accurate communication method God uses today, but it is also the most "fuzzy." It is hard to describe precisely what a "senser" is, because this type of communication is harder to quantify and measure than seeing or hearing. But it is also the easiest for most people to respond to because it is very similar to human intuition.

Sensers sometimes flow in this method without realizing they are hearing and obeying God. It just "seems natural" or "feels right," so they do it without pondering and resisting. In fact, many Christians who think they are "intuitive" may really be hearing God's voice and responding to Him.

Sensers often seem to have an incredible sense of timing. Somehow they just know to be in a certain place at a certain time. They seem to have an incredible number of divine appointments. They are known for being in the right place at the right time. Amazing things seem to "just happen" to them on a regular basis.

For example, a senser may feel prompted to telephone someone at just the right moment. From time to time, I need to talk with an individual who does a great deal of ministry traveling. He is seldom home. Yet, just about every time I need to reach him, I just "happen" to call on the one day out of a whole month when he is home. I never seem to have any difficulty reaching him. In fact, I did not realize that most people found him difficult to reach until one day when I happened to catch him in a very tight window between flights.

I had been meaning to call him for a few days, but never got around to it. One day he came strongly to my mind, and I felt prompted to call him right then. So I telephoned him, and he answered. He told me, "I can't believe you caught me! I just flew in this morning from Chicago. I am only home for five hours, and then I leave again for three weeks." God had prompted me to call him at just the right time.

Here is another example of divinely orchestrated timing. One Christmas morning several years ago, I woke up at 5:00 A.M. and started wrapping the last of my presents. Suddenly I felt strongly prompted to call Joyce, an elderly friend of mine. She was in her sixties at that time and taking care of her ninety-year-old mother.

I looked at the clock … 5:15 A.M. How could I possibly call someone at that time of day, especially on a holiday? The prompting was so strong that I could not ignore it. I resisted the notion for about fifteen minutes, and then I finally picked up the phone and dialed. I decided to let it ring twice and hang up if she did not answer. Joyce was a sound sleeper, so maybe the phone would not wake her.

She answered on the first ring. That meant she was up and sitting on her sofa in the living room, next to where she kept her phone. Her voice was tearful as she said, "Hello."

"What's wrong?" I asked her.

She told me that she and her mother had planned to spend Christmas with her recently widowed sister, Patty. Neither Joyce nor her mother drove, so Patty planned to pick them up and take them to her house. But late the previous evening, Patty called with bad news. Her car had broken down, and she could not get anyone to fix it because it was a holiday. Joyce and her mother could not afford a taxi, so Joyce had been up all night crying and asking God somehow to make it possible for her to go to her sister's for Christmas.

I had a very busy day scheduled myself, with a house full of relatives arriving. Since we talked so early, I was able to make arrangements to pick up Joyce and her mother at 7:30 A.M., drive them to Patty's and get home in time for my company. They spent the night at Patty's, and I picked them up the next day and took them home.

God had prompted me to call at that outrageous hour in response to Joyce's prayers. If I had listened to the dictates of common sense and waited until a more reasonable hour to telephone Joyce, it would have been too late to help them get to Patty's house for Christmas. This is an example of the divine timing in which sensers frequently seem to move.

The Lord leads sensers in subtle ways. The leading is not always as immediately obvious as getting a picture or hearing God speak to you, but it is every bit as sovereign a communication from God.

God also shows sensers how to figure things out. Sometimes a senser will wonder how to do something and begin praying about that matter. Suddenly that person will have insight or an approach to use to figure out a solution. The approach will probably be innovative and brilliant. But that person did not figure it out alone—God gave the critical hints needed.

God has worked that way with me. One time was in regard to my ministry of providing online prophetic training. I had been using several computer chat room mechanisms to communicate with my students, including IRC, ICQ and AOL. I discovered that the average person who desired to receive my prophetic training was not technically savvy about chat rooms. It was very confusing for most of my students to have to learn how to install and use these complex programs on their computers. AOL's chat rooms were easy to use, but they required that people purchase AOL service. Some of our students could not do that. I began asking God for a workable solution—something free, universally available and easy to use. At the time, everyone thought ICQ would become the industry standard, but I felt that program was too complex for our average student to install and use.

In the meanwhile, as I looked for a solution, I encountered information about free AIM chat room software. AIM was not yet a well-known program at that time. Instinctively I *just knew* in my spirit that AIM was the way to go—but I could not explain why I knew that.

I used AOL on my personal computer and knew it was possible to create links (easy shortcuts to other sites) to AOL chat rooms. But AIM did not seem to have an equivalent procedure. No one (including AOL tech support) seemed to know how to set up links to private, frequently used AIM chat rooms.

One day I was having a combination prayer and technical meeting with Paul, one of my staff members. As we experimented with the AIM software, we alternated between doing technical work for the ministry and praying. During that time, we asked God to help us figure out how to use the AIM technology for His glory.

Suddenly an idea occurred to me, and I mentioned it to Paul. Together we worked on it as both of us received technical insights from God. Between us, we figured out a simple procedure that anyone could use to create a link to our chat room. Each time we paused to pray, both of us found ourselves thinking of new ways to do technical things.

As a result, we published the simple procedure we developed during that session, and many of our students have been able to join us on the simple and free AIM chat room. Shortly after that, Netscape began distributing AIM software as part of the Netscape release, and AIM became the industry standard for chat rooms. Our students no longer had to upload AIM from the Internet—it "came" with their computers.

However, we still had a subset of highly nontechnical people who could not follow our simple instructions and get to our chat room. One of them wrote to me repeatedly, asking me to e-mail a link to the room. As far as I knew, that was not possible. I did not know anyone who knew how to create a link to a specific AIM chat room.

One day as I prayed about it, God suddenly told me to go upstairs to my computer. There I began fidgeting with some things. Suddenly I received the insight to figure it out. After about twenty minutes of working on it and experimenting with the results, it was working perfectly.

God had shown me what approach to take to solve the problem. It was something I never would have figured out on my own, because it would have never occurred to me to take that type of approach. God dropped the strategy into my lap. But I had to do the legwork to actually get it working. God does this a lot with sensers; He shows them how to figure things out, and He gives them the hints they need to be successful.

INCORPORATING NATURAL ABILITY

Often the methods God reveals to sensers seem closely aligned to each person's natural ability. Since this is the way God works, it is vitally important for sensers to be able to sort out whether it is God who has revealed a matter or just their own intuition or skills. Sometimes God will piggyback a supernatural enablement on top of the sensor's natural ability, allowing that person to excel supernaturally at something for which that person already has an aptitude.

Joseph and Daniel are two Bible characters who demonstrate how God works in this way with sensers.

Joseph was sold into slavery at a young age, yet God prospered his work until he was given authority over an entire household of Egyptians. Even when he was falsely accused and thrown into prison, he ultimately received authority to administer the whole prison. Eventually he was released from prison and became a top political figure, second in the nation to Pharaoh in power and authority. Genesis 39:3 tells us that God "made all he did to prosper in his hand."

Daniel was a highly qualified individual when he was taken in captivity to Babylon. The Bible describes Daniel, and those taken with him, as "young men without any physical defect, handsome, showing aptitude for every kind of learning, well informed, quick to understand, and qualified to serve in the king's palace" (Dan. 1:4, NIV).

Yet Daniel, along with his three friends, purposed to take a stand for God. As a result, God gave them more understanding and wisdom than any of their peers:

> To these four young men God gave knowledge and understanding of all kinds of literature and learning. And Daniel could understand visions and dreams of all kinds.
> —DANIEL 1:17, NIV

God supernaturally heightened their natural abilities.

He piggybacked His anointing on top of their skills. God does this with sensers.

This is not to say that if you are a senser, God will always make you excel at everything. He probably won't. But it is not uncommon for God to cause a senser to excel from time to time at something that He wants done. It is as if God shows them how to do it better and smarter.

SUPERNATURAL KNOWLEDGE

At times God will suddenly deposit a large volume of specific detail into a senser's understanding. It may be in regard to a situation or person to whom you are ministering. One minute you don't know anything about that person. Then suddenly you know tons of information, perhaps details of past experiences that person has had. It is as though God had dropped an encyclopedia into your understanding. You know many details about that person—and all of the details are correct.

In short, God has given you supernatural revelation about a person or situation, but He has not explicitly told you what to do with the information. With sensers, God frequently gives them information and then leaves it up to them to decide how best to use it. (Of course, if you are stuck, James 1:5 still applies: If God gives you information and you don't understand what to do with it, then ask Him for wisdom or for a strategy. He will give it to you.)

One time a close friend was very upset about her mother, and the Lord told me to comfort her. This friend and I had never discussed her mother before. I knew absolutely nothing about her mother in the natural. But as I began to comfort her, I suddenly "just

164

knew" several specific details. I knew the mother had been deeply hurt in her late twenties and had fallen into bitterness. I knew the bitterness was the source of several health problems, including ulcers, high blood pressure and a heart condition. I knew that the mother was abrasive and difficult to talk to. I also knew that she could never be pleased. No matter what anyone did for her, it was never enough. I also knew that the mother was lonely, frightened and unable to trust anyone. All of this information just popped into me. One minute it was not there, and the next minute it was.

God did not specify how He wanted me to use these details. My friend is an intercessor, so I chose to present it to her as a prayer strategy. I suggested she pray for the Lord to empower her mother to release bitterness and to forgive the person who had hurt her so deeply when she was in her late twenties.

"That's true," my friend replied. "She never has gotten over that. She is consumed with bitterness."

Then I went on to talk about her mother's health problems in specific detail, relating that they had arisen out of the bitterness. Again, my friend acknowledged the health problems as though we were discussing something I knew about in the natural. We discussed how her mother's earlier disappointment and hurt had made her unable to be pleased and unable to trust. We talked about how God wanted to heal her mother's emotional pain and give her His peace.

I was able to give my friend insights into her mother's behavior, and she went away with a renewed resolution to intercede for a breakthrough for her mother. The next day she telephoned me, asking how I knew all the details about her mother. "When we were talking yesterday, it didn't occur to me how much you knew," she told me. "But after I slept on it, I realized you knew many specific details that I had never told you." She realized how the hand of God had been guiding our discussion on the previous day, and it encouraged her greatly.

When you are first learning to perceive what God is showing you, you may not get a lot of specific details. Instead, you may get hunches and general direction or basic insights. But it will come to you in this way: You will suddenly know or realize something that you had no way of knowing in the natural. When you notice this happening, begin to talk with God about it. Ask Him for more details or more insights. Ask Him for a strategy to best use the information He has just given you. The more you go back to God and interact with Him on what you get, the more you will fine-tune your hearing.

PROMPTING A SENSER TO ACTION

God will also prompt sensers to do or say something. They will not know why they should do or say this, but they just feel an urge—*a knowing*—that they should. Sometimes that prompting will be gentle and subtle. Other times it will be very intense. Sometimes it will be counter-intuitive, like when I called Joyce at 5:30 A.M. on Christmas day. But usually when the Lord is prompting us, we have a confidence and assuredness inside of us that it is the right thing to do.

Sometimes a tangible sense of God's presence accompanies the prompting. At other times there is an intensity that grows on us if we resist until it begins to overwhelm us. God will orchestrate the circumstances in order to make it very easy to flow with Him in the prompting you have received. For instance, God may prompt you to fly across the country to help a chronically sick relative. As you make your plans to go, you may discover a low-cost, round-trip ticket sale that the airline is having for just the one day on which you are purchasing the ticket.

Sometimes you will have just a little piece of the instruction. The rest will not come until you are "in motion." God doesn't tell us more until we start to act upon the instruction we have already received.

One time I was taking a two-week, intensive anthropology class at Fuller Seminary. During these intensive classes, the students have two main activities—participating in the classroom or studying. You may get a little sleep on the side, but mostly you go to class and study. There is only one weekend during the course, and students use every minute of it to study.

During my time in the class, I was staying with a friend who lived in a dorm apartment on campus. On Saturday about noon as I studied, I had a sudden, intense prompting to go outside. I tried to ignore it, figuring that it was just my own mind trying to get out of studying. But the intensity increased until I could not stand it. "Is this from You?" I finally asked God.

As if in response, I began to sense the Lord's presence with me. So I told my friend that I'd be back in a bit, and I went outside. I had absolutely no idea where I was going, just outside. As soon as I got outside, I knew I was supposed to go to the coffee shop on campus. It is closed on Saturdays, so the prompting was counter-intuitive. But I decided to go anyway.

It was about a ten-minute walk. When I got there, I looked around and saw nothing, and I felt no further prompting. I sat down on the steps and said, "God, You have five minutes. If You don't show me what You want me to do in the next five minutes, I am going back to my

167

studies." Then I waited. When I looked at my watch, four of the five minutes had passed. I closed my eyes to pray and ask God to show me what He wanted me to do.

"Excuse me," a voice interrupted my prayer. "Can you tell me where this dormitory is?" I knew where it was, but it was tricky to find. My five minutes were up, and God had not shown me anything. So I decided to walk with the man who questioned me over to the dorm, and then go back to my studies. We chatted as we walked.

He was coming to apply for the doctorate program in psychology offered by Fuller. I asked him what church he went to, and he replied that he did not go to church. I said that it was unusual for a Christian to not go to church. He replied that he was not a Christian. It had never occurred to me that someone would apply to a seminary and not be born again.

I shared the gospel with him—the first time he had ever heard it. As we spoke, I realized that he was my divine appointment. The reason God had sent me outside was to meet this man and share the gospel with him. God did this by unfolding it instruction by instruction. At first He simply prompted me to go outside. Once I was outside, He prompted me to go the campus coffee shop. Then He brought my divine appointment to me. I did not recognize him as a divine appointment at first. But as things unfolded, I fell into God's plan and was able to share the gospel with him.

It is not uncommon for God to lead sensers in that way. He does not always give us a full understanding of what He wants. Rather, He unfolds the next step as we obey the part He has already shown us. As we follow Him, He orchestrates some incredible things, but they often start out seeming rather mundane and nondescript.

BE SURE IT IS GOD

Having said all that, I need to give you a warning. It won't be God each and every time you have a hunch or feel prompted to do something. Sometimes it really is just us. Occasionally it is the enemy who is trying to mislead us. There may be a learning curve during which time you learn to tell God's promptings from others. I know I went through one. When I first started moving with God, I assumed that any open door was from Him. But not all open doors are from God. Over time I have learned that when it is God, I will usually have a deep confidence in what I have sensed, I will have a burning intensity, or I will sense the presence of God.

When it is not God speaking to me, I will often get a hesitancy or a bit of a check in my spirit. God may use another method (hearing or seeing) to correct me before I move out too far on the prompting. I have learned to pay a lot of attention to those checks in my spirit and to proceed slowly and prayerfully when they occur.

If you are a senser, invite God to orchestrate your day, guide you and show you His will. You may want to make this a daily prayer. I believe that is what the Lord desires us to do, as evidenced by Proverbs 3:5–6:

> Trust in the LORD with all your heart, and lean not on your own understanding; in all your ways acknowledge Him, and He shall direct your paths.

God will lead (or direct) sensers through promptings, but He really does expect us to look to Him for direction consciously and deliberately. We are not to follow every whim that comes along. We are to seek Him on a regular basis. He is to be the One who directs our paths. King David understood this and committed himself regularly to the Lord for direction. Psalm 37:5 instructs us to "commit [our] way to the LORD, trust also in Him, and He shall bring it to pass."

A WORD OF KNOWLEDGE

Another type of communication God uses is a word of knowledge. A word of knowledge takes place when God shows someone something about the condition of another person. He does this because He wants to minister to the need of that person. The most common form of the word of knowledge relates to physical ailments that God wants to heal. But He also communicates through a word of knowledge about emotional issues and specific situations.

If God wanted to give a *hearer* a word of knowledge about a stomach or digestive problem, He might say the words "stomach problem" or "digestive disorder." If He wanted to give this word to a *seer*, He might show the person a diagram of a stomach from a medical book, or He might show an image of a person holding his tummy and looking as if he were in pain. But if God wanted to give the same word of knowledge to a *senser*, most likely He would let them feel briefly the pain in their stomach.

If He wanted to give a senser a word of knowledge about a headache, He would allow that person to feel the headache. If the word of knowledge was about someone's intense anxiety, a senser may suddenly be overcome with anxiety for a brief period for no apparent reason.

I do not want to develop the concept of a word of knowledge and how to minister through this gift in this chapter. But it is helpful to note that when a senser gets a word of knowledge, it is usually a physical or emotional sensation. If you suddenly experience one of these sensations, and it does not seem to be appropriate to your circumstances, it may be a word of knowledge. God may be showing you someone else's pain because He wants you to minister to that person in some manner. He may want you to intercede for that person. Perhaps He wants you to pray with the person for a physical healing. If you get a word of knowledge and don't know whom it is for or what to do with it, ask God.

Peter Wagner taught the first course I took at Fuller Seminary, one on the subject of healing and praying for the sick. As a part of the course, each day in class Peter demonstrated praying for the sick. He began by getting a word of knowledge. Then he asked the person with that condition to come to the front of the room, and he prayed for them.

At the time I knew about deliverance and demons, but I had never heard of words of knowledge. As Peter prayed for a person with back pain, my own back began to hurt intently. Then he prayed from someone with a stomach condition, and my own stomach became intensely painful. I thought that spirits of infirmity were being cast out of the person that Peter was praying for and then were coming to me.

After class, I went up to Peter, convinced that I needed deliverance prayer. He asked me to explain why, and then broke into laughter when I shared my experience. I did not think it was funny, and I must have looked offended. Peter apologized for laughing and then explained to me about physical words of knowledge. He invited me to join him in praying for people in class the next day.

The next day as we prayed, I realized that I felt the pain another person was dealing with for a bit, and then it would go away. At the same time that my pain went away, the person for whom we were praying reported that his or her pain also left. Since then I have prayed for and ministered physical healing many times. Most of the time when God gives me a word of knowledge for healing, I experience it as a brief physical sensation in my body. I don't know why God communicates in that way, but He often does so with sensers.

TASTE AND SMELL

God communicates to people through the senses of taste and smell, but it is less common than through touch or sensing or "just knowing." Most of the time taste and smell are related to the discerning of spirits. Discerning of spirits is the ability to sense God's presence in a situation and to understand how He is operating in that situation. It is also the ability to sense the enemy's presence and method of operation in a situation.

People have reported smelling the "fragrance of the Lord" at meetings where God's presence was unusually strong. Some report the smell of roses. Others report the smell of frankincense and myrrh.

I don't operate in smell or taste very often myself. But in 1994, during the "Toronto Blessing," I traveled to Toronto to attend the services. The ministry team prayed for me during an evening service, and I soon lay before the Lord at the altar, enjoying the presence of God in my life.

The church operated a little coffee shop called "Joel's Place" just off the main sanctuary. That night as I lay in God's presence, the shop was baking cookies to sell the next day. The smell of baking cookies filled the sanctuary, and God's presence seemed so tangible. I could really sense the Lord right there with me. He met me in some wonderful ways. Since then, occasionally I have smelled the fragrance of the Lord in meetings where God's manifest presence entered the sanctuary. For me, the smell was not roses or frankincense—it was the smell of baking cookies, a smell I learned to associate with the Lord's presence while I was in Toronto.

Discerning of spirits is not limited to sensing the Holy Spirit's presence. We can also discern enemy activity in that way, often manifested by taste or smell. Those who operate in a deliverance ministry sometimes report the recognition of demons that smelled like rotten eggs or sour milk. The smell alerted them to the presence of the demons. Some have reported a bitter taste in their mouths during deliverance ministry.

One general consensus among those who operate in smell/taste in the gift of discernment is this: The enemy's presence smells or tastes bad or unpleasant. But God's presence smells or tastes good.

SCRIPTURAL EXAMPLES OF SENSERS

The Bible gives us some examples of sensers, just as it did with hearers and seers. Jonah was a senser. After he ran from God to a ship headed out to sea, a storm arose, and the sailors asked Jonah what they should do to appease the storm. The Bible does not record God sending an angel to converse with Jonah. He did not have a vision. Instead, he "just knew" what had to be done, something highly unusual and counter-intuitive. Jonah knew that he had to be thrown into the sea (Jon. 1:8–12).

I believe Jonah received this information directly from God, that the Lord spoke to him by depositing this information directly into his spirit. And Jonah's information was correct, because the storm ceased the instant he was thrown overboard (Jon. 1:15).

Daniel was another senser. He "knew" through Scripture. God revealed prophetic insights to him when he read the "writings of the prophets." God quickened the Scriptures to him, and suddenly he just knew how to apply them to his current situation (Dan. 9:1–3). Daniel launched into a very powerful identificational prayer of repentance. His prayer paved the way for the Jews to return to Jerusalem and for the temple to be rebuilt. The Scripture did not tell Daniel that identificational prayer was needed. Instead God prompted him to do this in response to reading Scripture.

Nehemiah was a senser. In fact, we see the gift of discernment operating in his life. In Nehemiah 6, some men were plotting against Nehemiah. They wanted to destroy him. Verse 2 says, "they were scheming to harm me" (NIV). In the midst of this situation, a prophet came to Nehemiah and gave him a false prophecy. The prophet said that God wanted Nehemiah to shut himself up in the temple and lock the doors to avoid being murdered that night (v. 10). If Nehemiah had done that, he would have lost the respect of the people he was leading and would have been rendered an ineffective leader.

Instead, God deposited supernatural revelation in Nehemiah's spirit (vv. 12–13). No one told Nehemiah what was going on in the natural. Instead God deposited the information into Nehemiah's spirit, and he "just knew" what was going on. Nehemiah described it this way:

> I realized that God had not sent him, but that he had prophesied against me because Tobiah and

Sanballat had hired him. He had been hired to intimidate me so that I would commit a sin by doing this, and then they would give me a bad name to discredit me.

—NIV

Elisha appears to be yet another senser. There are many amazing stories about Elisha, demonstrating that he "just knew" what he should do. Elisha did many very unusual things, and they worked out gloriously.

In one illustration, a barren Shunammite woman made a home for Elisha, and God rewarded her with a son. But when the miracle baby was a youth, he suddenly complained of head pain and died. The woman ran immediately to Elisha.

It is clear in the story that Elisha did not know everything about the situation, because he did not know why she was distressed (2 Kings 4:27). Elisha questioned her, and then she told him about her son. He rushed to her house, having no time to stop to pray and seek God for insight on what to do. The Bible does not record God speaking to him, sending an angel, giving a vision or any other type of direct revelation. But it does give us the following details:

> When Elisha came into the house, there was the child, lying dead on his bed. He went in therefore, shut the door behind the two of them, and prayed to the Lord. And he went up and lay on the child, and put his mouth on his mouth, his eyes on his eyes, and his hands on his hands; and he stretched himself out on the child, and the flesh of the child became warm. He returned and walked back and forth in the house, and again went up and stretched himself out on him; then the child

175

sneezed seven times, and the child opened his eyes.
—2 Kings 4:32–35

This story reveals that Elisha just knew what to do. We also see that his revelation was progressive. He got a partial revelation, and the dead child's flesh became warm. Then he got up and paced back and forth. I believe his pacing demonstrated the intensity in him. The same intensity accompanies the "just knowing" or "prompting" God drops into a senser's spirit.

Then God dropped a bit more divine revelation into Elisha's spirit. He acted on it, and the dead boy was restored to life.

In another biblical example in the life of Elisha, he "just knew" the strange things to do to make a poisoned stew safe to eat. (See 2 Kings 4:38–41.) A group of prophets came together for a season. As they made a stew, one of them dumped poisonous mushrooms into the stew, and no one realized it until they had already eaten part of the stew. Panicked, they came to Elisha for help.

Elisha took a handful of flour and dumped it into the stew. Supernaturally, the stew was made good. Now, in the natural we know that flour is not an antidote for poisonous mushrooms. And even if it was, how would adding it to the stew have countered what was already in the people's systems from eating the poisoned stew? Instead of looking for a natural reaction or antidote, Elisha "just knew" that God wanted a prophetic gesture of purification. God did not tell that to Elisha directly—He dropped that divine revelation in Elisha's spirit. We can confirm that Elisha's divine intuition was correct, since no one died from the poisonous mushrooms.

Let's look at one last story from 2 Kings 2, occurring

just before Elijah was taken up into heaven without dying first. Elisha knew Elijah would be taken, and he refused to leave his side despite several requests to do so from Elijah. Finally, Elijah asked Elisha what he wanted. Elisha asked for a double portion of Elijah's anointing. Elijah appeared surprised by this request, and told him that he was asking for a hard thing (v. 10). But right then, in the midst of a discussion where Elisha had Elijah's undivided attention, Elijah does not take time to seek God—nor does God speak to him.

Elijah simply replied to Elisha, "Nevertheless, if you see me when I am taken from you, it shall be so for you; but if not, it shall not be so" (2 Kings 2:10). How did Elijah know to say that? I believe this is another case where God plopped the revelation into his spirit, and he "just knew."

We know how the story ended. A chariot of fire separated the two as they were walking. Elijah was taken up to heaven in a whirlwind, and Elisha does, in fact, see it happen. Elijah's mantle dropped down to Elisha.

> Then he took the mantle of Elijah that had fallen from him, and struck the water, and said, "Where is the LORD God of Elijah?" And when he also had struck the water, it was divided this way and that; and Elisha crossed over. Now when the sons of the prophets who were from Jericho saw him, they said, "The spirit of Elijah rests on Elisha."
> —2 Kings 2:14–15

Elijah "just knew" to say something that sounded really off the wall. Like Elisha, he was a senser. As the subsequent events unfolded, his words were confirmed and his sensory communication from God proved to be accurate.

POINTS TO PONDER

1. As you look back over your past, have there been times when the Lord may have led you through promptings and you did not realize that He was leading you at the time? Can you describe one such instance?

2. Have you ever had an experience where the Lord seemed to expand your natural ability in an area to accomplish something for His purposes? Or have you had a time when He showed you how to figure something out after you asked Him for help?

3. Has God ever dropped a sudden insight, understanding or piece of knowledge into your spirit? Maybe you suddenly realized why someone behaved in a certain way, or you suddenly knew how to find someplace without having clear directions with you. Have you had any other experiences along those lines?

4. Have you felt that strong certainty in your spirit that God wanted you to do (or not do) something? What were the circumstances for that? Is that something you experience frequently, or is it a rare experience?

5. How can we go about discerning between God's promptings (which we should obey) and promptings from other sources that we should not obey?

6. Has God ever given you a "word of knowledge" for someone? If so, was it about a physical problem, an emotional state or a certain circumstance? How did God communicate this information to you?

THIRTEEN

When Things Go Wrong

No matter how good our hearing becomes, there will be times when we hear wrong or make a mistake. This chapter will take a look at what to do when we hear wrong.

WATCH OUT FOR "ALTERERS"

There are some things that can affect the accuracy of our hearing. I call these things "alterers," and we must learn to recognize them in order to avoid their effect upon hearing the voice of God in our life.

I know one lady who could hear God in an incredible way. But if she was really tired or exhausted, the accuracy of her hearing greatly decreased. Because she had high confidence in her ability to hear God—and was usually very good at it—it became dangerous when she was tired. If she did not notice when she was exhausted, she would make serious mistakes in communicating what God had said to her and would not be aware that she was making them.

One day, when she was rested and fresh, the Lord talked to her about how being tired altered her ability to hear accurately. He told her that she needed to do a "self-check" a few times each day to see if she was getting fatigued. She became aware of how fatigue affected her hearing. The self-check alerted her to when her hearing might be suspect.

Other alterers are things like worry, lack of peace, fear, anxiety, distance in our walk with God or sin in our lives. It is good to get in the habit of doing a regular self-check in these areas with God. We need to know when we are vulnerable to making a mistake or mishearing God. If we are aware of the presence of an alterer, we can adjust accordingly and continue accurately hearing God.

David prayed a prayer in Psalm 139:23–24 that I encourage you to pray daily. He said:

> Search me, O God, and know my heart; try me, and know my anxieties; and see if there is any wicked way in me, and lead me in the way everlasting.

In short, David examined his heart before God on a regular basis. We need to do this, too. The more frequently we examine our hearts before God, the less likely it is that anything will be able to separate us from Him or to interfere with our hearing.

CHECK YOUR RELATIONSHIPS WITH OTHERS

Our relationships with others can also affect our hearing. If we harbor unforgiveness, bitterness or hate toward another person, those feelings can hinder the clear flow of our hearing, and we will be susceptible to hearing wrong.

Jesus clearly warned us against harboring unforgiveness in our hearts. In fact, in Matthew 18:32–35, Jesus tells us that the Father will deliver us to the "tormentors" for unforgiveness. In other words, the enemy gains a foothold in our lives when we refuse to forgive or when we harbor bitterness.

One of the ways these tormentors torment us is by imitating God's voice. They pretend to be God, and they tell us things that are not really of Him. Don't allow them to get a foothold in your life. If you don't seem to be hearing God accurately, one of the very first things you should do is to look for any sin or unforgiveness in your life. If you find it, deal with it immediately.

RECOGNIZE YOUR HEARING PATTERNS

After you examine your heart before God and rid your life of anything that could give the enemy access, begin to look for patterns—patterns that help you to hear better and patterns that hinder your hearing. You can become alert to the hearing patterns that help you to hear clearly. And you can also distinguish the patterns that hinder you and cause you to hear wrong.

Each time you hear God speak, ask these questions: What did it sound like? How did God communicate that information to me? How do I hear Him most clearly? Learn to recognize the patterns He uses to speak to you.

For instance, when I began checking my own hearing patterns, I found that the "deep knowing" was almost always correct. Almost every time I heard God wrong, it happened to be that "still small voice" that sounds like my own thoughts. Although I usually hear God correctly through that still, small voice, I am more susceptible to inaccurate hearing through that hearing pattern. Most of the time I hear God accurately. But if I am going to make a mistake, it will probably be when I hear the "voice" that sounds so much like my own thoughts.

The patterns that hinder you from hearing God clearly may be different from the patterns that hinder me from hearing his voice. One key to learning to hear God accurately is to know your own patterns! Pay attention to how God sounds when you hear accurately, and recognize the hearing pattern when you do not hear accurately. You can also ask yourself the following questions when you discover that you did not hear accurately: Was I tired? Was I bored? Was I busy? Was I angry? Did I sense a check or a confirmation in my spirit? Did I feel a sense of confidence when I heard this, or was there a check in my spirit? Do I tend to mishear more frequently on any specific topics or subjects?

If you are concerned about the accuracy of your hearing on a given topic, then you might want to bounce what you "hear" off someone you trust and with whom you have a good relationship. It might be your pastor, an elder or leader in your church or a prayer partner. Also, go back and review chapter 9 ("What God's Voice Does Not Sound Like"), and eliminate those types of things.

EVALUATE THE CRITICALNESS OF THE COMMUNICATION

Occasionally God talks to me about "heavenly things"— a term from John 3:12. Jesus talked to Nicodemus about being born again, and Nicodemus, not comprehending what Jesus was saying, asked Him, "How can this be?" In essence he was saying, "I don't understand; please explain it to me."

Jesus replied to Nicodemus, "If I have told you earthly things and you do not believe, how will you believe if I tell you heavenly things?"

I ask God about heavenly things all the time. Mostly He ignores me, but occasionally He explains things to me. Sometimes He chooses to tell me something about how things are done in heaven. This information doesn't really affect my life or my daily Christian walk; it is purely informational in nature. It does not matter if I heard right or not, because it does not have much of an effect on me.

On the other hand, when I think God has given me a directive that will be "expensive" to obey, it is important for me to sort out whether or not the directive really came from God. In other words, there are times when it is more critical to know for sure whether or not a word is from God. There are other times when that is not so important.

For instance, one time God told me some details about how angels carry out their tasks. To tell you the truth, I am not positive if that was God or just my thoughts. I think it was probably God. But even if it was my own thoughts, it really does not matter, because the topic was heavenly information. It does not affect my walk with the Lord to know how angels carry out an

183

assignment. Therefore it is not worth my effort to try to sort out whether this was God speaking to me or whether it was my own imagination.

There are many times when it is crucial to know a word you have received came directly from God. But my story about the angel illustrates that at other times it is not so important. The key is carefully assessing each situation and determining how important it is to know whether you have heard clearly. Once you have determined that, then pursue it accordingly.

JUMPING TO THE WRONG CONCLUSIONS

There will be times when you hear God accurately, but make assumptions and jump to conclusions about what He said that are wrong. Sometimes God gives us partial information. When this happens, most of us try to fill in the blanks from our own understanding—often by making assumptions. Bill Hamon did that when God told him that He would protect that which was most precious to Bill. Bill's daughter was in grave danger, but Bill was unaware of that, so he assumed God was talking about the property. In the end, he lost the property—but his daughter's life was spared.

Bill heard God clearly, but he attached the wrong meaning to what God said, jumping to inaccurate conclusions about what God meant. Bill Hamon is respected and recognized internationally as a man who hears God very well. If a man of that stature and caliber can occasionally make assumptions that lead to a misunderstanding of what God said, then so can the rest of us.

Jesus addressed this in one of His parables. He knows

us well, and He knows our tendency to make assumptions and jump to conclusions. In Matthew 20:1–16 He spoke about a landowner who hired workers for his vineyard. They agreed on a wage for the day and went to work. A few hours later, the landowner hired some more workers who agreed to work for whatever was reasonable. Throughout the day, the landowner continued to hire more workers. When the day was over, the workers who only worked a few hours were paid the same salary as that agreed upon by the workers hired first. The original workers had assumed that they would be paid more since they had performed a greater share of the work. They were upset when they received precisely the agreed-upon wages.

Assumptions can interfere with the accuracy of our understanding of what God actually meant when He spoke to us. Sometimes when it seems that you have heard wrong, that isn't really the case. Maybe you heard God clearly, but you jumped to some inaccurate conclusions about what He meant. You might want to go back to see if you made any misleading assumptions.

UNDERSTANDING GOD'S TIMETABLE

There is one final area where we can make a mistake. We may hear God clearly and accurately, but misunderstand His timetable. In other words, we may look for fulfillment of His word to happen immediately, but God was talking about something that would happen in the future—next week, next month, maybe even next year. If we fail to understand God's timetable and the situation doesn't work out immediately the way we expected it to after hearing God, we decide we have heard wrong. But then later on, God fulfills His word in His perfect timing. When we look back, we realize we did not mishear after all.

On one occasion I was ministering in upstate New York. As I prayed for a lady, God began to speak to me about her. I repeated to her the things God said. For nearly fifteen minutes I continued praying for her as God spoke to me about many areas of her life. Then He began to talk about her family rejecting her because she was a believer. He said that He would cause those relationships to be fully restored, so she must not become discouraged.

As soon as I said that she stopped me. Up to that point she had agreed with everything I had said. But that last part did not sit right with her. She said that her whole family was unsaved, but they were a very tight-knit family. She got along well with all of her sisters and all of their spouses and children. She had not experienced any rejection from her family for being a believer, so she felt I had heard God wrong on that.

The next day she came back to me in tears. Her family had sent a letter to her by courier, signed by her parents and all her brothers and sisters, telling her they were sick of all her talk about Jesus. They said they did not want to see her unless she promised not to mention Jesus again. She was devastated. Just as she was about to slip into despair, she remembered what I had shared the previous night. God had promised He would restore the relationships after her family rejected her. It had not made sense at that moment, but now it did.

The night before, we thought I had heard wrong. It

turns out that I had heard accurately, but we had misunderstood God's timetable. But as she stood there holding that letter, God's words to her were a great comfort.

Sometimes God does that. Sometimes He is speaking of future-tense events, and we tend to interpret them in the present tense. What He says may be confusing because it may not line up with our experiences at the moment, but it will make sense later on.

POINTS TO PONDER

1. Why do you think that things like unrepented sin and bitterness can interfere with our ability to hear God clearly?

2. Have you noticed any patterns in your own life of how and when God speaks to you? If so, what are they?

3. Are you aware of times in your own life, or in the life of a friend, when you heard God's voice but jumped to a wrong conclusion about what He meant? Can you think of any examples from the Bible of God's people doing that?

FOURTEEN

How to Fine-tune Your Hearing

There must be a million "self-help" books on every topic from how to improve your golf swing to how to make friends and influence people to how to improve your memory. All of these books have one element in common: They all share information and then have you practice applying it. Many self-help books contain specific exercises to help you practice and improve your skills in the topic of the book.

The same thing applies to learning to hear God's voice. We can fine-tune our hearing by practicing. That is what this chapter is about. It explores ways to increase our accuracy in hearing God and recognizing His voice. When I first started, I was only about 50 percent accurate. Over time, God took me through a process of "refining" my hearing. It became easier to hear God, and I also found I became much more accurate in my hearing. I would like to share some of the techniques that God used with me. I think you might find them helpful.

REVIEW YOUR DAY WITH GOD

One of the first things God started doing was having me review my day with Him. I am not a night person. I am a morning person. So each morning when I woke up, I had a quiet time with the Lord before I got out of bed. The Lord asked me to review my previous day with Him. When I first started doing this, it was mostly a case of going back to review my day mentally. As I did, I asked God how He felt about this or that.

But as time progressed, the Lord began speaking to me more and more. He would tell me how He was pleased with this, or how I had missed His leading in that. Sometimes He would tell me how I had inadvertently hurt someone's feelings by what I had said and would send me back to them to apologize. Over time, God began taking more and more of the lead in the process of reviewing my day.

I no longer do this every single day, but it is a common practice for me to review my day with the Lord. He talks to me about areas where I heard Him clearly. He also talks to me about areas where I missed it. He points out attitudes or mind-sets that I have to work on. He shows me areas where He has caused me to grow and become stronger in Him. Often He also gives me a direction and strategy for the upcoming day.

This quiet review time with God helps me to become more aware of how He speaks to me and leads me. You might want to start doing this as well. If you are a night person, you might want to do this at night just before you go to bed instead of in the morning when you wake up.

CONFIRMING HIS WORD TO YOU

God asked me to complete simple little exercises that I call "confirmations." He would speak to me about something simple and easy to observe or confirm. I would hear Him tell me the information, and then I would immediately observe that it was correct. This began to build confidence in my hearing. This is not something you can initiate. It is something that God initiates. The more receptive you are to God, the easier it will be to facilitate the process.

For instance, suppose you are about to walk into a grocery store, and you think to yourself, *The lines will be unusually long today.* You can choose to discount and ignore the thought. Or you can ask God, "Lord, is that You speaking to me? If so, what else do You want to say to me?" Invite God into the process; enter a dialogue with Him. When you get inside, look at the lines. One of two things will occur—either you heard right, or you heard wrong.

If you heard right and the lines are long, become proactive in the process. Talk with God. Thank Him for speaking to you. Ask Him if He has anything else to say, and then pay attention to what He shares.

If the lines are not long, you heard wrong. You can still be proactive with God. Go back to Him and say, "Lord, I thought You said...but I heard wrong. Please speak to me now about this. Why did I hear wrong? What can I do to improve my hearing?" Invite God to help you hear Him more clearly.

God loves to be invited into your hearing and into your day. Even if you start way off in left field, you can invite Him in, and He can turn things around to His glory. Be alert. Look for the possibility of God's speaking to you in the little things. If you think you heard God, invite Him into the process. Observe the results of what you heard, and then dialogue with God about it.

You can talk with God whether you "heard right" or "heard wrong." Ask Him to fine-tune your hearing. Invite Him into the process, and He will come.

ASK GOD WHAT HE THINKS

You can also question God about the things you believe He is saying to you. When you see a headline in the newspaper about something that bothers you, stop to ask God how He feels about it. Ask Him how you can reflect *His* attitude and not your own. When you drive through specific areas in your city, ask God what His heart and strategy is for the people in that area. Invite Him into all your experiences and activities.

Ask Him to talk to you about a wide variety of subjects. Pay attention to what you see, hear, feel or perceive—it may be God answering you. Don't try to limit God's response because He may answer you in a way that is totally unexpected to you.

A verse of Scripture may run through your thoughts, and that verse could be God's response to your question. You may suddenly be flooded with a brief sadness, which God allows to show you His feelings about a situation that you are facing. God may speak to you through His still, small voice in your thoughts. Or He may give you a picture or an image.

DEVELOP INCREASED INTIMACY WITH GOD

Remember that your personal intimacy with God affects your hearing. The better you know Him, the easier it will be to hear His voice. So if you want to fine-tune your hearing, you need to develop increased intimacy with God. One of the best ways I know to increase that intimacy is to spend more time with God.

I am not talking about reading the Bible or listening to worship tapes or interceding for your friends and community. All those things are an important part of everyday Christian life, but I am talking about consciously and intentionally inviting God into your activities. Let me give you a few examples.

Invite God to watch the movies you watch with you. (This can be dangerous if you watch the wrong type of movie.) I like action and adventure movies. Sometimes I get interested in one that begins to have violence, sex or bad language in it. On more than one occasion, even though I became interested in a movie, God has said, "I don't like this one. Turn it off."

God will often watch a show with me and chat with me during it. This is very similar to the way you might sit on the sofa with a friend to watch television and chat about it from time to time. This is spending time with God and fellowshiping with Him by including Him in your "nonreligious" activities.

I remember the days when the San Francisco 49ers were the Superbowl champions. In order to get a ticket to a game, you had to be a season ticket holder. Ed and I are football fans, and we wanted to go to some of the games, but tickets simply were not available. The Lord prompted an acquaintance of ours to bless us by giving us their tickets to a game they could not attend.

We discovered we had very good seats—on the fifty-yard line about twelve rows up. The game was wonderful, and I found myself enjoying it immensely. During halftime, I began thinking about how good it was of God to give us these tickets, so I thanked Him for them. Almost as an afterthought, I invited Him to sit in the seat next to me and enjoy the game with me.

To my surprise, God accepted the invitation. I had a mental image of Him sitting in the seat next to me, which happened to be unoccupied. He had His arm around my shoulders, and He was holding a hot dog in His other hand. The image was funny, and I laughed. God laughed with me. I could really literally sense His presence beside me, and it made the game even more enjoyable.

Suddenly God began to tell me what was going to happen on the next play. "It is going to be a running play, and they will gain seven yards." Or, "There will be an interception on the next play." The game had been exciting before. But it became even more exciting as I watched to see if the play worked out just the way God told me it would. It always did!

This was an incredible experience, one that left me feeling closer to God than I had before. Such experiences allow you to spend intimate time with God. Invite Him into the activities you enjoy. Invite Him to be a part of them with you. Include Him and be mindful of Him.

PRACTICAL HEARING EXERCISES

The following practical exercises will help to increase the clarity and accuracy of your hearing. If you have computer Internet access, there is a resource that contains many other wonderful and helpful exercises.

It is the website for my ministry—GodSpeak International. The Internet address is www.godspeak.org. Please check this site out; it contains many helpful resources.

EXERCISE 1

Similar to journaling, this exercise asks God to speak directly to you. Write down what you "hear." Don't try to sort it out or to evaluate it while you write. At a later time, prayerfully go back over it and evaluate it. But first, ask God to speak to you. Spend time listening to what He has to say.

This exercise allows you to practice listening to God. From time to time, some of your own thoughts may sneak in. That is OK, because you will later go back and evaluate what you heard. But listen and record what you heard first. Use the following ideas to record what you hear:

- Get paper and pencil and write it out by hand.
- Sit at your computer and record the message in your favorite program.
- Use a typewriter.

The important thing is to find the format that is most comfortable for you. Some people do this best when they play a worship tape quietly in the background. Others find it works better to find a quiet spot and complete silence. Use whatever method works best for you.

Invite the Lord to speak to you. Take authority over Satan and forbid the enemy to interfere in this exercise. Spend fifteen to twenty minutes "listening" to God and writing down what you hear. He may speak to you conversationally. If so, write what He says. He may recall verses or portions of Scripture to your memory. If so, jot them down. He may show you a picture. If so, draw it or describe it. You may be overcome with some sensation, like joy or peace. If so, spend a few minutes enjoying it, and then write yourself a note about what you experienced. If you do not think that you are hearing anything from God, then jot down whatever thoughts are going through your mind.

When you think you are done, ask God if there is anything else He would like to say. Wait a few minutes for Him to respond if He wants to do so. When you are sure God is finished, go back and prayerfully read what you have written down.

INVITE THE LORD TO SPEAK TO YOU

Invite God to be involved with you in the process of sorting this out. Invite Him to speak to you as you review what you wrote down. Then begin to run it though some filters. Cross out anything that is unscriptural or that contradicts the Bible. Cross out anything that is harsh and condemning. God may convict you of sin or areas of rebellion in your life, but Romans 8:1 tells us that He will not condemn us.

Go back over your work, and prayerfully read it again. It is very likely that God will speak to you some more as you read it.

The following form can be used to complete this exercise. Begin with the prayer, and then complete the form.

Name: _____

Date: _____

Father, I believe I have a deposit of Your presence within me through Your indwelling Holy Spirit. My body is the temple of the Holy Spirit. Father,

You have said for us to come boldly to Your throne and make our requests known to You. Lord, I am asking You now to speak to me briefly about some area of my life. Tell me an area where You would like to bring your presence or victory, or show me a strategy or plan You have for my life.

I am going to believe You for this. I will write what I hear You say to me. Lord, let what I hear be sanctified and pure. May it represent what You have chosen to say to me at this time. I thank You in advance for answering my prayer. I give You the praise and the glory for what You are doing in me now. In Jesus' name I ask these things. Amen.

Lord, I believe You are saying to me . . .

_____

_____

_____

_____

_____

EXERCISE 2

This exercise is similar to exercise 1, except that you are going to ask God a series of specific questions that target areas of your life. The exercise takes three weeks to work through. Each week you spend fifteen to twenty minutes daily asking God specific questions and listening and recording His answers

Do this for five consecutive days. On the sixth day, prayerfully review what God spoke to you on each of those five days. On the seventh day, ask God if there is anything else He would like to say to you in the area you are targeting that week. In other words, ask Him

a *general* question instead of a *specific* one.
Week one of this three-week series targets learning
to understand your own heart. The second week targets your relationships with others. The final week
targets your relationship with God.

Begin each day with a prayer similar to the prayer
below.

> Dear Lord, in the name of Your Son, Jesus Christ,
> I come before Your throne. I am washed by the
> blood. Christ lives within me. Not just in part, but
> in my whole being. I bring every thought of my
> mind and soul into captivity to the mind of Christ.
> I will listen to what You have to say to me. I trust
> You to communicate with me. As I am writing, I
> will not question what You have said. I will write
> it down as I hear it, and then I will trust You to
> confirm or correct it later when I prayerfully
> review it with You. I am a believer, and I expect to
> receive. I thank You for speaking to me.
>
> In the name of Jesus, by His power and author-
> ity, I take authority over every demon and inter-
> fering spirit. I forbid any enemy activity in this
> exercise. Satan (and any of your demons), you
> may NOT interfere in this or imitate God's voice
> to me as I open my heart to hear the Holy Spirit.
> I take authority over fear, anxiety, doubt and
> unbelief in the name of Jesus, and I command you
> to leave now. I bind any negative, critical or con-
> demning spirit in the name of Jesus and forbid
> you to interfere or to imitate God's voice to me.
>
> Lord, please come and be in charge of all that
> happens here. Please speak clearly and power-
> fully to me. Amen.

Use the following questions for each day of the three-week period:

Week 1—Our own heart

Day 1: Lord, what do You see as my greatest strength? And how would You like me to use it for Your glory?

Day 2: Lord, what is my area of greatest weakness? How can I best work with You to get stronger in this area?

Day 3: Lord, please show me the spiritual gifts You have given me. How can I learn to be more effective in using them to do what You are doing?

Day 4: Lord, what do You think is my greatest fear? How can I put that under Your lordship so that You might work Your glory in that area of my life?

Day 5: Lord, please speak to me about the call and destiny You have on my life. Why did You put me here on this earth? How can I best serve You?

Day 6: (On this day, prayerfully review what God spoke to you on days one through five.)

Day 7: Lord, is there anything else You would like to say to me regarding the topic of knowing my own heart and thinking patterns?

Week 2—Our relationship with others

Day 1: Lord, would You please reveal to me the areas in my own heart where I do not love myself or where I am unable to receive Your love, especially in the areas where it affects my relationship with others? Also, will You show me how You really feel about me in these areas?

Day 2: (Think back over your life and the person or experience that most deeply hurt you—or choose one if there were many. Invite the Lord to speak to you about that situation, how He felt about it, how He can work His glory in it and whether or not there are still areas where you need to forgive or release bitterness or be healed of pain.)

Day 3: (Ask the Lord to review the past two weeks with you and to point out two things to you—those times when you acted in His love toward someone, and those times when you reacted to someone in the wrong spirit. Ask the Lord to show you any patterns in your interactions with others that He would like to change.)

Day 4: Lord, please show me if there is anyone whom I am hurting or treating poorly or misjudging. Please show me Your heart for that person.

Day 5: Lord, please reveal to me one or two people whom You have strategically placed in my life to be a blessing to me or to help me grow. Please show me how best to receive from You through them. Please also show me how to be a blessing to them.

Day 6: (On this day, prayerfully review what God spoke to you on days one through five.)

Day 7: Lord, is there anything else You would like to say to me in the area of my relationship to others?

Week 3—Our relationship with God

Day 1: Lord, what are the areas of my life where You want lordship, but I have not given it to You yet? Would You please select one and show me how to put the area You have selected under Your lordship?

Day 2: Lord, what is the thing that most pleases You in our relationship together?

Day 3: Lord, is there any area of my life where You desire to work more of Your holiness in me? If so, how can I best cooperate with You in that?

Day 4: Lord, please show me how You have been speaking to me during my day over the past few weeks. How might I be able to recognize Your voice even more quickly?

Day 5: Lord, how can I please You more? How can I bless You? How can I draw even closer to You?

Day 6: (On this day, prayerfully review what God spoke to you on days one through five.)

Day 7: Lord, is there anything else You would like to say to me in the area of my relationship with You?

Once you have heard from the Lord in these areas, you may desire to prayerfully review with Him what He said to you. You may want to use that as a "launching pad" to dialogue with Him about these areas of your life.

FIFTEEN

Empowered to Hear

When I share my testimonies and stories of how God speaks to me, some people think that I am special or unique. They tell me, "I wish I could hear God like you do." Well, the good news is that you can! There is not anything special about me that permits me to hear God's voice more clearly than any of the rest of God's children. Everything that I've shared in this book is material that God intends to be a part of normal everyday Christianity. It is for all believers.

I took God up on His offer to teach me how to hear His voice, and He did! He is making the same offer to you. God wants to talk to you just as He talks to me. I know for a fact that if you sincerely take Him up on His offer, He will teach you His voice. He loves doing that.

I have been teaching people how to work with God to learn to hear His voice for the past five years. These people come from different walks of life and different parts of the globe. Most of them are ordinary, everyday Christians. They are students, or they hold jobs and have families. They have learned to hear God for themselves. He speaks to them regularly, in the big stuff and also in the routine items of their day-to-day lives.

I asked a few of them to share some of their success stories on hearing God in this chapter. I wanted to share their stories with you because I would like you to be encouraged.

If I can learn to recognize and discern God's voice, so can you! If these people can learn to hear God for themselves, you can do it too!

DOROTHY GOODMAN
TEXAS CITY, TEXAS

Dorothy is a sixty-eight-year-old saint who decided to return to college. In addition to classes, she also worked in the physical education department as a student worker. One day she noticed a young lady about to leave the gymnasium through a door that would set off the alarm. She went to the woman to stop her, and they ended up in a conversation. The Lord began to give Dorothy information and words of knowledge about this woman, including details about her life and the things with which she was struggling. The information included details about some nightmares the woman was having.

Dorothy shared the information God had given her, and the woman was astonished. She was particularly amazed that Dorothy, a total stranger, knew about the nightmares she was having. The woman became very receptive to the gospel after realizing that God knew all about her. Dorothy offered to pray for the young woman, who asked Dorothy to pray for her *right then and there* in the gymnasium.

DIANE THOMAS
LONG BEACH, CALIFORNIA

I went through a long battle with my mother, who was in her seventies and had cancer of the stomach. It was heart-wrenching. I remember when she passed away at the hospital. Her passing was real quiet and peaceful, but when we knew she was gone, we all cried. I was left alone with her "earth suit." We were really close, and I began to despair very much. In fact, I felt as though I would lose it. Then, very loudly, in my mind the Lord said, "Diane, to be absent from the body is to be present with the Lord." From that moment on I was changed. I had joy that was unreal. As I helped with all the others involved, I realized that it was purely a supernatural intervention.

JOHN WALKER
ERWIN, NORTH CAROLINA

I am reminded of an incident that occurred many years ago when, as a teenager, I lived in New York City. One day as I left the apartment to board the subway, I realized that I had only two fifteen-cent tokens—nothing more: one token for my ride to work, the other to pay my fare back home. Silently, I prayed for a financial blessing. As I left the street to enter the station, I walked past a piece of folded leather. Once inside the station, repeatedly I heard a quiet voice saying, "Go back to the street and pick up that leather." Thinking, *How silly to use my last token on such a thing*, nevertheless I obeyed. Inside that simple piece of folded leather was approximately a week's pay!

CAROLYN CRITCHER
KNOXVILLE, TENNESSEE

I was driving down the interstate in a hurry because I was late to a meeting at the university. It was raining. I suddenly became aware that I was following the car in front of me too closely. I thought, *I should slow down.* But I argued with myself, thinking, But, I'm late... *Yes, it's raining, and it is not safe to be this close to the car in front of me...But, it's OK.*

Finally I took my foot off the accelerator and fell back slowly. Immediately, the car I was following hit water, lost control and spun 360 degrees, ending on the shoulder safely. My car and the other nearby cars were barely able to brake without losing control. We all avoided collisions. Had I still been following too closely, a multi-car pileup would most likely have ensued.

With adrenaline flowing, only then did I recognize that *the Lord* had called to my attention the fact that I had been driving dangerously. His grace helped me win the argument with myself, allowing me to do the right thing and slow down.

LISA MONTALVO
PENSACOLA, FLORIDA

The Lord is teaching my husband and me to hear His voice more clearly all the time. Often the Lord gives my husband, who is in ministry school, and me the same word at about the same time. We will ask each other, "Did the Lord give you anything?" It is awesome to discover that almost always the Lord has given us the same thing. It's God's way of saying, "Yes, you are hearing Me."

One day we stopped to help a young man who was trying to take home a lot of groceries with only a bike. Some of his bags fell, so we took them home for him. I heard the Lord say, "Give him twenty dollars." I thought it was just me. After a little time went by, my husband said, "I felt the Lord say to give him twenty dollars." We just looked at each other, knowing then that we had heard God once again, and yet we questioned our hearing.

ERMA KUMMERER
FOSTORIA, OHIO

My story happened a long time ago before I knew how to hear clearly from God. Our family was attending a Father's Day picnic at a park down the road from my house. I needed to go home to get something for the picnic, so I took my two-year-old daughter with me. I pulled up beside my house, left Jenny in the car and left the car running. I knew I would only be in the house for five minutes at the most. I figured Jenny would be fine; she was too little to have enough power to do anything.

While I was in the kitchen getting what I needed, I heard God speak to me clearly and emphatically, "Get that child out of that car!" I thought I was imagining things, so I finished up what I was doing and went to the car. It was gone—baby, car and all. I was in an immediate panic. I ran down the alley screaming for someone to help me. I couldn't think clearly.

Finally, a neighbor man, who looked up and down the alley and around the block, found Jenny near the grain tank at a mill just one block away. She was standing beside the wheel in the car, and she was fine. God protected her as she "drove" the car straight down the alley where it stopped by the grain tank in the next block.

If the car had not gone straight, she would have hit a garage, shed or tree. God had mercy on me even though I didn't listen to His warning.

JANICE AYEW-EW
DAVENPORT, IOWA

Janice lived in Bethlehem, Israel, in 1983 and 1984, a time period when that nation was plagued with constant bombings and shootings. One day she needed to go to Jerusalem for the afternoon, and planned to go by Arabic bus. As she waited for the bus in Bethlehem Square, the Lord spoke to Janice and told her to go check on a blind friend who lived down the road.

She needed to go to Jerusalem to do her job, so she hesitated. But the Lord seemed to be tugging on her heart, so she decided she had better obey His prompting. She went to her friend's house and then went home afterward.

That evening as she listened to the news she discovered that the bus on which she would have been riding had she not obeyed God had been bombed en route to Jerusalem. Three people were killed. The Lord had protected her by keeping her off that bus!

CATHY COLLIE
BURNS LAKE, BRITISH COLUMBIA, CANADA

When my daughter was about eight years old, she was playing hide-and-seek with our next door neighbor's girl. As I vacuumed in the house, suddenly this thought popped into my mind: *Go outside on your sun deck.*

I obeyed, and there, hanging over the edge of the sun deck railing, was my daughter. (Our sun deck is ten to twelve feet off the ground.) She was screaming her head off, but I never would have heard her in the house over the noise of the vacuum. If I hadn't obeyed the Lord as He spoke to me in my thoughts, my daughter would have been seriously hurt. But God protected her by warning me.

LINDSEY PRATT
WAYLAND, MICHIGAN

One day I dropped my Bible in the church parking lot. It got all muddy, and the binding broke; I was very upset that it was falling apart. A few days later I went to the store to get another. I found what I wanted at the nearest Bible store—a pink leather, slimline New International Version Bible. Oh, it was wonderful.

I also wanted to get my husband a study Bible. But I soon discovered that even if the Bibles were to go on sale, they still would cost *way* more than I could afford. It was almost Christmas, and we have four children, so I decided to just tape my broken Bible and wait.

However, I simply could not get the Bibles out of my mind. I wanted them very much! One day shortly afterward, I was grocery shopping when the Lord spoke to me. He told me to get out of my car and go into one particular flea market/junk store. That word didn't make a lot of sense to me, so I sat there for a minute pondering whether that had really been God's voice speaking to me. I wanted to drive home, but that prompting would not go away.

Finally I got out of the car and went into the junk store. Just inside of the door was a table with a pile of books. There sitting on the top of the pile—just waiting for me—was a pink leather Bible, just like the one I had seen in the store. Right next to it was a beautiful study Bible. Both were in perfect condition, as if they were still brand-new. They were there for me, and they cost all of two dollars or so. God gave me the Bibles I wanted at a price I could easily afford.

HADA CATRICOLA
ALLENTOWN, PENNSYLVANIA

Hada's son went to Bible college in Southern California, clear across the country from her home. He needed a job to pay expenses, and he asked her to pray for him. In response to her prayer, the Lord gave Hada a picture of a men's shoe store on the second floor of a mall, to the right of the escalator.

She did not know what to do about it, so she told her son about the picture she got. The son went to the mall, and sure enough, a men's shoe store was located right where she saw it in her mind. Her son chatted briefly with one of the employees, who said it was a wonderful place to work, but they seldom hired new people because everyone loved it there so much that no one ever quit. He went back home and called his mother. Hada felt strongly impressed of the Lord to tell her son to go back there and apply for a job. So he did.

The same day that he put in his application, an employee left and he was immediately hired.

RALF TOBI
AMSTERDAM, THE NETHERLANDS

Ralf and his wife were living in Sweden, and they felt called of God to relocate to Amsterdam. They went by ferry, and en route they started to pray and ask God where they were to live. As if in response to their prayer, the name "Johan" came to Ralf's mind. Johan was a Christian leader whom they knew who was currently living in Amsterdam, but they had not been in contact with Johan for quite some time.

Ralf wanted to tell his wife about his thoughts. "I have a strange thought…" he began, but before he could finish the sentence, his wife said, "Johan!"

This did not make sense to either of them because they knew Johan had a very large family and would not have room for two houseguests over an extended stay. For a few days they stayed with another friend.

One day Ralf ran into Johan, who was looking for someone to stay in his house and take care of it while he and his family went on vacation for seven weeks. This gave Ralf and his wife plenty of time to find an apartment and get comfortably settled.

AMARILYS FLORES
SAN JOSE, COSTA RICA, CENTRAL AMERICA

I had been having a hard time hearing the voice of the Lord, and when I asked Him why, I felt He told me it was because I had been too busy doing other things and was physically tired. So I went to sleep and got refreshed. That week I lost a set of keys from the house. I couldn't find them and started to worry because I couldn't remember where I had put them.

209

After several days I still hadn't found them. I asked the Lord to help me find them, and He showed me that I had left them in my laboratory right next to a basket. I went there, and just as He said, the keys were there.

MICHELE EDWARDS
EMILY, MINNESOTA

Several years ago I was part of a woman's prayer group that met every other week. During one meeting, a lady came who asked prayer for her daughter who was going through a very difficult time. The daughter was struggling with deep depression and feelings of low self-worth. Even though I had never met the daughter, we prayed for her for several weeks.

Some friends of mine (not the same ones who were in the prayer group) and I planned to go out to eat at a small restaurant in our city. When I arrived at the restaurant, I glanced briefly at a woman who was sitting all alone at the counter. We sat down to eat, but the whole time we were eating, the Lord kept drawing my attention back to the woman at the counter. God spoke to me, telling me to go over to her and, "Tell her how much I love her!"

I did the normal thing for me to do—I kept arguing with myself about whether it was really God or just myself. As the prodding became stronger and more evident, I realized that this was truly God. I excused myself from the table and approached the woman in fear and trembling!

Nervously I cleared my throat and said, "Excuse me." As she turned around I could see deep sadness in her face. Encouraged to continue speaking by the sadness I saw in her face, I sat down beside her and said, "I don't normally do things like this. But the whole time I have been here, I have felt that the Lord was telling me to come and tell you how much He loves you!" My words opened the door, and I was able to minister the love of God to her, right there in the restaurant!

I left, feeling that God had deeply touched her, but as we drove away, I realized that I didn't even get her name!

The next time our prayer group met, the mother who asked us to be praying for her daughter was there. She was very excited to share a praise report with us. She had just talked with her daughter the day before. Her daughter told her that she had been going through a particularly hard day, to the point where she was seriously contemplating suicide. In her depression she had gone for a walk, and then decided to stop at a little restaurant to get something to eat. While she was eating, a lady she didn't even know came up to her and told her how much Jesus loved her!

We all rejoiced for her. It took me a while, but I finally realized that the woman who talked to her was me!

DEBI BRISTER
THERMOPOLIS, WYOMING

A few years ago, my husband and I were struggling financially. One night, a young man came to our house wanting to sell us encyclopedias. It was very cold outside and light snow was falling, so we invited him in just to warm up.

Although we had no intention of buying anything, we felt sorry for this young man. We thought we might as well let him practice his selling presentation on us. As he was nervously presenting his product, I was nervously hearing the Lord tell us to bless this young man financially. He got to the bottom line where we were given the opportunity to purchase this set of books.

I told him that I would like to talk to my husband in private before we made any commitments. We excused ourselves to another room, and I told Eddie that I felt the Lord had told me to give this kid some money. He said that the Lord told him the same thing.

At that time we were not walking in an abundance of finances. I looked in my billfold, and we discovered that we had a twenty-dollar bill and a fifty-dollar bill. I heard the Lord say, "Do you want a twenty-dollar blessing, or do you want a fifty-dollar blessing?" We agreed to give the fifty dollars.

When we returned to the table, we explained to the young man that we were not going to buy the encyclopedias. His disappointment was all too obvious. We then told him that the Lord told us to bless him, and we handed him the money. He began to weep.

We discovered that he once knew the Lord, but had turned his back on Him. He poured out his heart to us. We led him in returning to God. He told us that his mother prayed for him all the time, and she would be so happy to hear that he got things right with the Lord.

LINDA ALLEN
FREEPORT, TEXAS

Conversing with God is an absolutely awesome adventure. The times I hear Him most are not when I'm in "prayer time"; it is when I'm just talking to Him during my day. A typical example of this is something that happened today.

I was looking for a receipt from purchasing tires for

my automobile. One of the tires developed a flaw, and I needed to take it back to be replaced. I looked every place I could think of—in all the normal places I usually put those types of things, and then every place I don't put those kinds of things. I checked the glove compartment, the console, under the seats and over the visor. I came inside and checked my file cabinets, drawers, my craft table, bulletin board—everywhere. Finally (I know from experience I should do this first and not last!), I said, "Lord, what in the world did I do with that receipt?"

Plainly He said, "Go look behind the glove compartment in your car." I went back to the car and pulled open the glove compartment. There was a small area where you could stick your hand from the bottom and back of the drawer. Sure enough, there was the receipt. Somehow, in opening and closing the compartment for different things, the receipt had been pushed out over the back of the drawer and was sitting under it.

DOUGLAS STERNER
MARTINSVILLE, NEW JERSEY

Doug experienced the Lord's speaking to Him through a strong prompting. He was at home, singing along with one of his favorite worship tapes, when he suddenly felt strongly impressed to go to the local Christian bookstore. Doug could not think of any reason to go there. It was a half-hour-drive away. He tried to ignore the prompting and go back to worship, but he simply could not get the idea out of his mind. The prompting was so strong it was almost a compulsion. So he finally decided to go ahead and drive over to the bookstore.

He arrived and began browsing aimlessly, wondering

what he was doing there. A few minutes later, he saw a rush of movement out of the corner of his eye. He turned and saw Mike, a close friend from his college days, running toward him. The college had been in another state, and they had lost contact with each other after graduation. They had a wonderful reunion.

Doug was even more surprised when he heard Mike's side of the story. Mike just happened to be in town that weekend and had to run an errand to a shop in another shopping center just across the street. He just happened to be in the parking lot when Doug drove by, and he looked up and noticed Doug's car. Mike was too far away to see the driver, but he thought he recognized the car as belonging to Doug. So he hopped into his own car and followed it. He saw Doug go into the Christian bookstore and went in to meet him.

FRANKIE MOORE
HALLAM, NEBRASKA

A neighbor I had once had recently come to America from Greece. The Lord enabled us to learn each other's language enough to communicate and become friends. With every passing day, we were more and more able to have brief conversations. One afternoon while I was having my private time of prayer and worship, the Lord told me to go to my Greek friend's house and tell her that I loved her. I tried to avoid doing what the Lord spoke, thinking how embarrassing it might be to approach her just like that and say, "I love you!"

Finally the leading of the Holy Spirit was so strong that I decided I must be obedient. I knocked on her door. There was no answer. I knocked again and still no answer. I said in my heart, " See, Lord, no one is home." But before I could walk away, the door swung open. My friend stood there looking very haggard. Her eyes were terribly swollen from crying. I knew something was drastically wrong. I explained to her that I had been at home praying and that God had told me to come over and tell her how much I loved her.

My friend broke out in heavy sobbing and held out her hand to me. I saw that within her grasp was a razor blade. She looked at me through her many tears and explained that she was so lonely, away from all her relatives and friends in Greece. She said that she had been ready to use the razor blade to take her own life—mainly because she felt no one loved or cared about her.

She threw her arms around me and thanked me for saving her life. I explained to her that God loved her so greatly that He had merely sent me to be an expression of His very own love for her. It was a wonderful opening for me to tell her about Jesus. Within a few moments, she was praying the sinner's prayer and asking Jesus to come into her heart.

GOD WANTS
TO SPEAK TO YOU

Did you enjoy these stories? Are you encouraged? Do you believe that you can begin to hear God as clearly and accurately as these people did? If you receive no other message from reading this book but this, I hope you will remember this one point: God wants to speak to you, and you can hear Him clearly!

Let me close our time together by praying for you:

Lord, I ask for Your blessing on these readers. Thank You that You have already given them ears to hear You. Now, Lord, release the understanding, clarity and discernment of Your voice. Give them even more of a heart to obey You. Draw them into deeper intimacy with You. Reveal Yourself to them even more.

Begin to give feedback and confirmation of the times when they are hearing You. Be faithful to give loving correction when it is needed so they will not inadvertently follow any other voice but Yours. Let them see how trustworthy You are and how capable and willing You are to communicate. Lord, fine-tune their hearing. Make it sharper, clearer and more distinct. Bless them with eyes to see, ears to hear and the ability to sense what You are doing. Lord, please orchestrate several successes for them in hearing Your voice. Bless them greatly. I pray this in Jesus' name, amen.

Notes

CHAPTER 2
GOD IS A COMMUNICATING GOD

1. Source obtained from the Internet: John Webster, "Hearing God's Voice," Prophetic-School Training 201, week 1 (Transforming Life Prophetic Ministries, 1999), www.godspeak.net/godspeak/201/lesson1.html.

2. Source obtained from the Internet: Donna Cox, Gary Cox, Jane Fitz-Gibbon, Sally Miller, Ira Milligan, Chris Poole, Teresa Seputis, David White and Jim Wies, "Is God Still Speaking Today?", Prophetic-School Training 101, week 3 (GodSpeak International, 1998), www.godspeak.net/godspeak/101/train_3.html.

3. Ibid.

CHAPTER 9
WHAT GOD'S VOICE DOES NOT SOUND LIKE

1. Source obtained from the Internet: John Webster, "The Lifestyle of Listening," Prophetic-School Training 201, week 4 (Transforming Life Prophetic Ministries, 1999), www.godspeak.net/201/lesson4.html

To contact the author
to speak at your church, conference or retreat,
please send your request in writing to:

Teresa Seputis
GodSpeak International
P. O. Box 423435
San Francisco, CA 94142-3435

You may also e-mail Teresa at this address:

Teresa@godspeak.org

Or you may call (415) 722-1013
and leave a message.

If you have Internet access, you may wish to check
out the GodSpeak International website. It contains
many excellent (and free) teachings and resources.
The website address is:

http://www.godspeak.org